MW00682770

Comments on other *Amazing Stories* from readers & reviewers

"*Tightly written volumes filled with lots of wit and humour about famous and infamous Canadians.*"
Eric Shackleton, *The Globe and Mail*

"*The heightened sense of drama and intrigue, combined with a good dose of human interest is what sets* Amazing Stories *apart.*"
Pamela Klaffke, *Calgary Herald*

"*This is popular history as it should be... For this price, buy two and give one to a friend.*"
Terry Cook, a reader from Ottawa, on **Rebel Women**

"*Glasner creates the moment of the explosion itself in graphic detail...she builds detail upon gruesome detail to create a convincingly authentic picture.*"
Peggy McKinnon, *The Sunday Herald,* on **The Halifax Explosion**

"*It was wonderful...I found I could not put it down. I was sorry when it was completed.*"
Dorothy F. from Manitoba on **Marie-Anne Lagimodière**

"*Stories are rich in description, and bristle with a clever, stylish realness.*"
Mark Weber, *Central Alberta Advisor,* on **Ghost Town Stories II**

"*A compelling read. Bertin...has selected only the most intriguing tales, which she narrates with a wealth of detail.*"
Joyce Glasner, *New Brunswick Reader,* on **Strange Events**

"*The resulting book is one readers will want to share with all the women in their lives.*"
Lynn Martel, *Rocky Mountain Outlook,* on **Women Explorers**

DISCARDED
PROPERTY OF
NEW HORIZONS SCHOOL

CHRISTMAS IN THE PRAIRIES

AMAZING STORIES

CHRISTMAS IN THE PRAIRIES

Heartwarming Legends, Tales, and Traditions

HOLIDAY

by Rich Mole

PROPERTY OF
NEW HORIZONS SCHOOL

PUBLISHED BY ALTITUDE PUBLISHING CANADA LTD.
1500 Railway Avenue, Canmore, Alberta T1W 1P6
www.altitudepublishing.com
1-800-957-6888

Copyright 2004 © Rich Mole
All rights reserved
First published 2004

Extreme care has been taken to ensure that all information presented in
this book is accurate and up to date. Neither the author nor the
publisher can be held responsible for any errors.

Publisher   Stephen Hutchings
Associate Publisher   Kara Turner
Series Editor   Jill Foran
Editor   Pat Kozak

We acknowledge the financial support of the Government
of Canada through the Book Publishing Industry Development
Program (BPIDP) for our publishing activities.

Altitude GreenTree Program
Altitude Publishing will plant twice as many trees as were used
in the manufacturing of this product.

We acknowledge the support of the Canada Council for the Arts which
in 2003 invested $21.7 million in writing and publishing throughout Canada.

Canada Council   Conseil des Arts
for the Arts   du Canada

National Library of Canada Cataloguing in Publication Data

Mole, Rich, 1946-
Christmas in the Prairies / Rich Mole.

(Amazing stories)
Includes bibliographical references.
ISBN 1-55153-782-6

1. Christmas--Prairie Provinces--History.
I. Title. II. Series: Amazing stories (Canmore, Alta.)

GT4987.15.M643 2004   394.2663'09712   C2004-903752-8

An application for the trademark for Amazing Stories™
has been made and the registered trademark is pending.

Printed and bound in Canada by Friesens
2 4 6 8 9 7 5 3 1

To Audrey, who lived this book with me.

Contents

Prologue

Furtively, silently, the hunched figures dart out from the shadows of trackside sheds. Canvas bags bouncing on their backs, they race alongside the high wooden sides of the moving boxcars, deafened by the squeal and clank of jostling couplings and revolving wheels. Praying that their half-numbed feet won't slip on the slush-covered ground, they glance over their shoulders at the oncoming cars. They lunge upwards, fingers clutching the ice-covered wooden rungs. Muscles straining, they lever themselves aboard.

Back in the shadows, still pressed against the shed, a trembling teenager watches the train speed away from him. Cold, hungry, and exhausted, he decides to stay put and take his chances in this city the "rods" have brought him to. "This is Winnipeg, isn't it?" he asks himself. "And it's Christmas Day. Not that one day is any different from the rest, but, maybe ..."

He knows there are houses not far from the rail yard. Warm houses. Houses where a kid might come in out of the cold, or at least get something to eat. He looks at the endless rows of stationary boxcars and figures the quickest way out of the yard would be to climb on top of one, then jump from car to car. He pauses and questions himself again.

Christmas in the Prairies

"But what if ya slip and break a leg? Who's gonna look after you?" Knowing the answer to that question only too well, he steps silently onto the tracks and begins weaving his way through the maze of cars. Once out of the yard, the solitary traveller turns up his collar, shoves his hands into his jacket pockets, and starts walking.

Chapter 1
Christmas in a New Land

F ree land! This startling offer from Canada captured the imagination and fired the hopes of people from all over Europe, Britain, and the United States. And so, in tens of thousands, they journeyed across oceans and strange lands to begin their lives again on the Canadian Prairies. Most of the newcomers who heeded that call brought little more than their memories, keepsakes, and traditions. These traditions — especially the traditions of Christmas — are still cherished in the great expanse of land now called Manitoba, Saskatchewan, and Alberta.

Filling the Last Best West

"Free land" was the marketing campaign — waged in many

PROPERTY OF
NEW HORIZONS SCHOOL

languages — that galvanized the restless and discontented to action. The Canadian government's public relations onslaught used every tactic imaginable, from agricultural fair exhibits (which sometimes included a stuffed buffalo), to somewhat fanciful periodical feature stories, to romanticized post-office posters.

Trainloads of American correspondents and editors were brought to Canada to see the bounty of the "northern" prairies for themselves. The lure proved irresistible to land-starved Yankees. Almost one million Americans responded to the government's offer.

In the hyperbolic and slightly condescending style of the era, a Saskatoon Board of Trade promotional piece told potential settlers in 1906, "It is not surprising that our farmers succeed so well: The crop never fails. Why, then, should the farmer? ... If a farmer here suffers crop failure, it is safe to say that the fault lies solely with himself [sic]. Crop failure can only result from laziness, carelessness or indifference to the correct and very simple methods of soil cultivation."

The mastermind behind the acceleration of the first of three enormous waves of immigrants, Clifford Sifton, used more sophisticated but equally effective rhetoric. By 1905, Sifton's Immigration Branch budget was a staggering $4 million. As the Dominion's marketing manager, he didn't have to lobby for the money. Filling the "Last, Best West" with settlers had become a national obsession. Sifton knew his target market: "... a stalwart peasant in a sheepskin coat, born on the soil ... with a stout wife and half a dozen children ..." The land-wise peasants came in droves, but so did shopkeepers, coal miners, and factory workers who knew little about farming and less about Prairie weather.

And so they came; between 1896 and 1914, some three million. In 1913 alone, a high tide of 413,000 immigrants washed over the Canadian Prairies. Initially stemming the tide, World War I later increased immigration. Unable to employ returning veterans, war-weary England offered them free passage anywhere in the British Empire. Thousands chose Canada.

Music and Meals of Home

The soaring sound slows pedestrians hurrying through their last-minute shopping on Christmas Eve. On the corner of a Winnipeg street, a young girl loading a disc into her CD player pauses, pulls the earphones from her ears, and looks up. Voices lifted in song float through an open window of an apartment above the storefronts. Few listeners can understand the words, but there is no mistaking the pure emotion in the lyrics.

It's the sound of a place that the singers' grandparents called home — a place where most of the singers themselves had never been. It's the sound of a *koleda*, a Christmas carol, whose evocative words and haunting tunes first floated over the snow-swept Manitoba prairie from thick earthen-walled soddies 90 years ago.

In the singers' modern apartment, there is an old sideboard. On the top shelf, in a space usually reserved for teacups, a traditional *szopka*, or manger scene, is displayed. In this apartment, and in the homes of other Polish descendants all over the Prairies, many other old-country traditions will be observed during the holidays.

Later on Christmas Eve — after the first star has appeared in the night sky — young and old will stand around the dinner table to say grace. The *oplatek*, an unleavened wafer stamped with the figures of the Christ child, the Blessed Mary, and the holy angels, will be shared amongst the group. The first *oplatek* will be offered by wife to husband. This is the "bread of love," so husband and wife will embrace and kiss. Everyone else will then do the same.

Glasses of *krupnik* (alcohol and honey), will be raised in a celebration toast. Then hosts and guests pass among them the dozen meatless dishes that represent the 12 apostles. First there is *barszcz* (beet soup) and *uszka* (dumplings and mushrooms), followed by jellied fish and some *golabki* (cabbage rolls stuffed with rice or buckwheat). Then it is on to fried carp, *pierogi* (dumplings stuffed with cheese or potatoes), and finally, fruit compote and baked sweets, such as poppy seed rolls or apple strudel.

Often, the meal is eaten by the light of two candles, each bedecked with blue ribbons. In some rural homes, hay will be strewn under the tablecloth to symbolize Christ's birth in a manger, and a sheaf of wheat will be placed on the floor near a window. In years gone by, that wheat would then be tied around the fruit trees to ensure a better crop the next summer.

Similar in many ways to the Polish traditions are the customs still observed by the descendants of Ukrainian immigrants. No time of the year is more festive than the Ukrainian Christmas season, which, when New Year and Epiphany are included, encompasses two weeks of feasts, carols, and special religious services.

Because the Ukrainian Orthodox Church still uses the Julian calendar, instead of the Gregorian calendar, Christmas Eve and Christmas Day fall on January 6 and 7. Although most modern-day families of Ukrainian descent observe Christmas at the same time as other Canadians, the older generation still celebrates on January 6.

At the Christmas Eve supper, two *kolachi*, circular braided loaves, create a traditional table centrepiece, complete with a central candle anchored in a glass of salt. As in the Polish tradition, the twinkling of the first star on Christmas Eve is the signal for the feast of 12 meatless dishes to begin. But farming families don't eat until the livestock have been fed! This is not the night to skimp when feeding the animals. Legend has it that animals are granted the gift of speech on this special day. That means they might complain to God if they feel slighted by owners.

The feast begins with Christmas *kutia*, a special sweet dish of boiled wheat, poppy seeds, and honey. The first spoonful is thrown at the ceiling for good luck, but the rest is kept for the diners. *Borsch* (cabbage and beet soup), *pryohy* (dumplings with various fillings), *holubtsi* (rice wrapped in cabbage leaves), as well as fish, cornmeal, sweet buns, and more fruit and vegetable dishes, ensure nobody goes hungry.

Christmas Eve is but the first of three days of the Ukrainian Christmas. After an early service on Christmas Day, feasting, carolling, and visiting continue for two days. There is more fun and celebration on *Malanka*, New Year's Eve.

The third major holiday is Epiphany (January 19), also known as the Feast of the River Jordan, to celebrate Christ's baptism. The night before Epiphany is called Generous Eve and is celebrated as a second Christmas Eve with its own traditional festive meal and the singing of *shchedrivky*, special Epiphany carols.

The traditional water-blessing ceremony, conducted on January 19 — often in bone-chilling temperatures — includes a solemn procession of singers making their way to a riverbank. Here, the priest blesses the water, and members of the congregation take jars of the blessed water home as protection against evil or to give to sick relatives or friends.

In the Prairie homes of German descendants, as well as in Mennonite and some Hutterite colonies, an evergreen Advent wreath graces the middle of the table for a month before Christmas. The wreath encircles four tall candles, three pink and one white. Every Sunday, another candle is lit — the first by the youngest child — until Christmas, when all the candles are replaced with white candles. Croatians place three candles in a bowl of four-inch-high grass; the candles represent the three wise men.

For Norwegians, Christmas culinary dishes include flat-bread, *lutefisk* (dry cod soaked in lye), and tasty bakery delicacies such as *fattigmand* and *julekake*. For the descendents of Icelandic immigrants, it is the succulent taste of *hangikjot* (smoked mutton) and perhaps the sweet indulgence of the prune-filled *vinar-terta* (Vienna tart) or *ponnukokur* (thin pancakes spread with brown sugar).

For the English, it is goose or turkey, plum pudding and mincemeat, followed by port and cheese. After the heavy meal, rounds of favourite carols such as "God Rest Ye Merry Gentlemen" are sung beneath garlands of holly and clusters of mistletoe.

These, then, are just a few of the many old-country traditions and treats. Thousands of kilometres, and more than 100 years distant from their origins, they are still enjoyed and cherished by thousands of Canadians.

Loneliness and Longing
Between the late 1890s and 1913, three million immigrants flooded into the Canadian Prairies. About two-thirds were from Europe and Britain, and a third from the United States. In spite of religious, linguistic, and cultural differences, almost all shared one common trait — loneliness. This was never felt more keenly than at Christmastime.

Christmas in the Prairies

Harry and Kathleen Strange first experienced loneliness at Christmas in London, long before the couple left England to come to Canada. It so happened that during the Christmas holidays of 1918, both Harry and Kathleen's families had left London. The young couple prepared themselves for a dismal, depressing Christmas Day. Depression turned to delight as they received a Christmas morning invitation to attend a reception, concert, and dance at the Royal Albert Hall.

As wonderful as the event was, it was the experience of turning a dismal day into something special that made an impression on them. When they immigrated and settled on a farm near Stettler, Alberta, the couple vowed to extend their own hospitality each Christmas to others who were far from home and family.

Many of the guests invited to their farmhouse provided unexpected surprises. Among the "succession of interesting, delightful and amusing strangers," Kathleen later recalled, was the grain elevator worker who turned out to be a Cambridge fellow and mathematician. Another guest, a lonely, disheartened, unemployed bachelor, turned out to be the scion of one of England's oldest families. Unfortunately, this blue-blooded fellow had trouble holding a job. Inspired by his place and time in his adopted country, he kept putting down his tools and picking up a pencil to immortalize his observations in verse.

Kathleen had some misgivings about another guest, a taciturn individual regarded by many as a severe and unapproachable fellow. In retrospect, it is easy to understand the man's demeanor. Life was tough; you had to be tough to survive. Yet, this grouch "was transformed by two glasses of port, into a most delightful dinner table companion and an intimate of the very best literature."

Sometimes, the hospitality unexpectedly revealed just how destitute the visitors really were. Imagine the shame and wretchedness of the young man who fell violently ill immediately after dinner. A doctor was summoned and the boy was bedridden for days. His malady was easily diagnosed. He had not had a real meal for weeks. Finally given the opportunity to eat his fill, his digestive system simply rebelled.

In an article for the *Lethbridge Herald*, Kathleen Strange confessed that, as appreciative as her guests might have been for the opportunity for good cheer and companionship, it was she and her husband who "probably had most of the pleasure."

A decade before Kathleen and Harry settled in northern Alberta, another English immigrant, Monica Hopkins, joined her husband, Billie, at their newly established ranch in Priddis, near Calgary. It was just a few months before Christmas and this would be her first Christmas away from home. Now that thousands of kilometres separated her from parents and siblings, she longed for a parcel from them — something she could open on Christmas Day — something that would make her feel they were not quite so far away. Much to her disappointment, her family's parcel didn't arrive in time.

"We had quite a lot of English parcels from friends, but they were not quite the same ..." Monica wrote to a friend. Happily, the parcels were at the Priddis Post Office when Billie went to look for them on Boxing Day.

"My parcels from home were lovely," she wrote. "Mother and Father still think that we are more or less on the verge of starvation and that we can only get the absolute essentials ... and I have no intention of disillusioning them at present."

Disappointment and Disenchantment

Not all Christmases were happy for immigrants in their adopted land. In fact, life was difficult for most newcomers. Many discovered the "free land" was not worth much more than the price they paid for it. The soil was unyielding, the weather unforgiving, and their Anglo-Saxon neighbours — and the government that had enticed them to Manitoba, Saskatchewan, or Alberta in the first place — were sometimes less than hospitable.

Old Colony Mennonites were one of the most disenchanted immigrant groups. Eager to escape enforced assimilation in southern Russia during the 1870s, they had been easily lured to the Canadian Prairies with the promise of free land and freedom — freedom to educate their children in their own language. A generation later, they faced the hateful prospect of assimilation once more, through the public school edicts and the threat of military conscription. By the 1920s, thousands of Mennonites had left Manitoba and resettled in northern Mexico.

The majority of European immigrants stayed, however, and dealt with the challenges of assimilating into Canadian society. These challenges included dealing with prejudice. A Ukrainian family that lived on the outskirts of Edmonton during the 1930s had an unwelcome lesson in this form of intolerance at Christmas — a time of year when they least expected it.

At the local elementary school, two young girls became good friends. Harriet and Olga were not only good friends, they were secret friends. Harriet loved her visits to Olga's Ukrainian household; visits she didn't talk about at home. What she especially liked were the Ukrainian folk songs that Olga and her parents sang. There were dances, too, performed in brightly coloured costumes to the music of fiddle and guitar. Harriet was fascinated. There was nothing like this in her staunch and staid British home.

As Christmas approached and their teacher began planning for the school concert, Harriet had an inspiration: why couldn't the two girls perform a folk dance? That meant she would be able to wear a costume, too! Harriet persuaded Olga, Olga persuaded her father and brother to provide the music, and both girls persuaded their teacher to include the dance on the program. Olga's grandfather began training the girls in earnest. What a surprise for Harriet's father, the girls giggled. A Christmas surprise! Yes, indeed, for Harriet's father was school board chairman.

On the afternoon of the big day, just a few hours before the concert, the chairman at last took the opportunity to examine the school concert program. It was something he had meant to do long before, but there had been more important matters to attend to ...

Harriet's father blinked and stared down at the program. Harriet? His daughter? Performing this European peasant dance? He dashed from the office and drove to the school. By the time he burst through the classroom doorway, he was seething. He ordered the stunned teacher to cancel the dance number immediately. Then he turned to Harriet and berated her in front of her classmates.

The pupils couldn't resist telling their parents about such a dramatic, shocking scene. Olga went home in tears. Her older brother had to be restrained from making an impromptu visit to the Chairman's office. Many parents were alarmed and dismayed. Many, but not all. It wasn't until early in the New Year that tensions eased enough so the two could resume their friendship, at least during class time.

Years later, two elderly women would tell their grand-children about the unexpected and unwelcome lesson of prejudice they learned at their school Christmas concert.

The Bachelor Party Tradition
In the newly established Prairie Provinces, where men out-numbered women two-to-one, the "Christmas bachelor party" soon became a welcome prairie tradition. But, before

the fun and the fellowship could begin, the bachelors had to travel long distances.

One such bachelor, John Wilson, a former newspaperman who had put down his pen and picked up the tools of the farming trade, had a homestead south of Prince Albert, Saskatchewan. Each homestead was at least 160 acres, so John's "next door neighbours" weren't exactly on the other side of the backyard fence.

Like John, most men travelled many kilometres in order to stave off the Christmastime isolation. There were no trappings at these parties — no Christmas tree or holly, no mistletoe, and, as John put it, "no girls to kiss under it." But the gatherings were made memorable simply by the fact that there were other people in the same room.

One year, after Christmas festivities and a few hours' sleep, John and his friends did their chores, and then, "the whole neighbourhood started on a round of visits which lasted till the New Year. Sometimes a bunch of a dozen or more of us would descend unannounced upon some unsuspecting bachelor just as he was preparing for bed and proceed to make ourselves at home in his shack. In case his pantry should not be well supplied, we always took some eatables along, as well as a few packs of cards and usually some kind of musical instrument."

In spite of all the revelry, it seems prairie people remained quite prudent. "When travelling on the prairie at night," John later wrote, "one is apt to get lost, so being careful people, we generally waited for daylight and breakfast before dispersing." Quite so.

The Cowboy's Christmas

On Christmas Day of 1893, a poem written by an anonymous contributor from High River, Alberta, was published in the *Calgary Tribune.* Titled "The Cowboys Christmas," it undoubtedly spoke to many bachelors on the Canadian Prairies:

> Here in this land of the Wild West,
> Away from sweethearts and lovers,
> Distance from the scenes of our childhood,
> Away from our old-fashioned mothers,
> Removed from the storm beaten cottage,
> Where ivy still tenderly clings,
> Our absence makes a broken circle,
> Whilst we are like birds, on the wing.
> Away then with dull care and sorrow,
> The years are hastening away,
> Why should we think of the morrow,
> Why not drink and be merry today.
> Then here's to health to our dear old folks,
> To the friends still loving and true,
> Here's health to the land of our fathers,
> And, Wild West, here's health to you.

The Words of Charles Dickens

Bob Cratchet, Ebenezer Scrooge, Tiny Tim — the names, and the characteristics they represent, are as familiar today as they were when Charles Dickens created them more than 150 years ago. When British immigrants packed their belongings to come to Canada, many tucked in a copy of Dickens' *A Christmas Carol* among the Christmas ornaments and keepsakes. The classic story was, and still is, a cherished part of the British celebration of Christmas, even though families today are more likely to watch the film version on television than dig out the book to read.

However, those hardy souls who settled the Prairies were without the easy entertainment of television, so they relished the tradition of a formal reading of Dickens' Christmas classic. Occasionally, though, the festivities themselves thwarted theatrical and oratory efforts.

Dickens' own son, Francis, was among the many men who endured the tedious, and sometimes tempestuous, ocean voyage to call the Canadian West his home. In 1876, while serving as a North-West Mounted Police inspector, Dickens was invited to Christmas dinner at Fort MacLeod, south of the area now known as Calgary.

Before dinner was served, Inspector Dickens sampled — liberally — the potent "Milk Punch." As dinner and drinking progressed, the good inspector began to feel the effects of the punch bowl. Having advance knowledge of Francis's attendance, a somewhat presumptuous guest produced a

Inspector Francis J. Dickens

copy of the famous book and asked the inspector if he would read a passage or two.

It was probably not the first request of its kind. There is no way to know for sure, but by this time it is likely that Inspector Dickens was heartily sick of his father's tale, and his association with it. Dickens rose unsteadily to his feet, looked balefully about the room, mumbled the immortal line, "God bless us everyone," and then collapsed back in his chair — much to the consternation of those who expected more from the son of the father.

Nellie McClung, the famous author who advocated for women's rights during the early and mid-1900s, told a story about a Dickens' reading that got an even chillier reception. In wind-swept Manitou, Manitoba, in December 1901, a well-educated English immigrant, a certain Frederick Vander, decided to offer "An Evening With Dickens —The Christmas Carol" in the Manitou Town Hall.

The draughty wooden building was heated — but scarcely so, on this particularly blustery night — by a solitary stove in the middle of the floor. The small audience huddled around the stove, and out strode Mr. Vander in formal evening attire. In true Dickensian fashion (for, in his later years, the famous author himself gave spirited readings throughout much of Europe and North America), Mr. Vander played all the characters of the story, and did so with enthusiasm. However, his challenging task was made even more difficult because he was in competition with the elements outside the hall, and with a diligent caretaker inside the hall.

This caretaker periodically upstaged the reader with a performance of his own, as he set about noisily feeding the fire with more fuel from the woodpile. Outside, the wind howled and the tin roof rattled. Inside, the fire crackled and the caretaker clanked and clanged. The hour grew late and the temperature dropped, but the performance went on and on. Finally, unable to endure the cold any longer, some members of the audience tip-toed out of the hall to make their way home. As they opened the door, an icy blast sent the rest of the audience shivering deeper into coats and mufflers. At this point, even the star of the show had shrugged on his coat and gloves.

That was when Mr. Vander realized he was no longer in competition with the caretaker. It seemed he had left also, taking the last of the firewood with him! The persistent performer picked up the pace of the story and released the remaining faithful patrons before they all perished. Those who endured the ordeal felt they had truly "entered the magic circle of the Dickens' fellowship."

Fellowship may have also been the sentiment behind the decision of two young men to read the seasonal classic to the celebrating patrons of Edmonton's Alberta Bar. Or perhaps it was simply the Christmas cheer the place afforded. In any case, on this Christmas Eve, in the early 1960s, future publisher, journalist, and poet Jon Whyte decided that he and a friend would perform a two-man Dickens reading at the watering hole. Would the bar's habitués appreciate young University of Alberta students actually reading *A Christmas Carol*? Could the two compete with — perhaps even contribute to — the friendly laughter and happy conversation of the bar's Christmas Eve patrons? They were keen to find out.

Stuffing his copy of *A Christmas Carol* into his coat pocket, Jon set off on that bitterly cold night with his friend, eager for a comfortable, warm-hearted evening of drinks and Dickens. It would have been better, he and his friend agreed, if they both had copies of the book. What were the chances of finding another copy, at this hour, on this night? As they hurried along 100th Street, they came across a newsstand. Miraculously, there it was: a paperback copy of *A Christmas Carol*! A propitious sign: obviously, this special event was meant to be.

However, on that fateful Christmas Eve, the two would-be readers never discovered if the patrons were Dickens fans. They never had the opportunity to savour the applause — and perhaps the free round of drinks — their performance might have earned. They never even managed to step across the bar's threshold.

As the two young men headed towards the bar, they heard the loud wail of fire engine sirens. Within minutes, the bar patrons had tumbled out into the cold to follow the chilling sound. The two university students did likewise. Before long, they could see the glow of the fire. The large Sterling Furniture Warehouse was an inferno.

Jon, his companion, and hundreds of other Edmonton residents braved the cold that Christmas Eve to witness one of the largest, most destructive fires in the city's history. Dickens might have brought a halt to talk and laughter inside the warm intimacy of the Alberta, but out here on the street, firefighters — and the blaze they were battling — were the showstoppers. Sadly, this particular Christmas Eve, Bob

Cratchet, Ebenezer Scrooge, and even Tiny Tim were all forgotten in the tangle of hoses, the pall of smoke, and the heat of the flames.

Chapter 2
The Prairie Christmas Concert

owhere else but the rural Prairies, it seems, has the tradition of the Christmas concert become such a critical thread in the social fabric. Today, sitting comfortably in our split-level suburban homes a few short minutes from the mall, or standing on the deck of our high-rise condo, gazing down at the city's Christmas lights, we might pause for a moment and wonder why that is.

A Tradition Begins

The "concert" was, in the beginning, a Christmas religious service. Travelling missionaries held their first services in houses on isolated ranches and farms. With the formation of school districts, services were held inside the small rural schools, simply because these were the only structures capable of holding more than a few people. In this classroom environment, it was only natural that, over time, children became active participants rather than passive spectators.

Later, with the construction of churches, the children's Christmas concert continued as a separate entity, still usually staged in the schoolhouse. The concert's religious anteced-ent was acknowledged by the centrepiece recitation and re-enactment of that long-ago eve in Bethlehem — a tableau complete with bed-sheeted worshippers, animals (some-times props, sometimes real), and a Mary, Joseph, and baby Jesus. However, it would take a unique combination of fac-tors to turn that special entity into a yuletide tradition.

Chief among those factors was rural prairie isolation. While the husband might have grumbled at having to hitch the horse to the cutter and drive "all that way" to the school on a chilly night, the wife likely considered it the special occasion it truly was. At last, a chance to get out of the house! At last, a chance to meet and talk with other women! The Christmas concert brought people together in a way that few other occasions did.

The Christmas concert was, then, both a social occa-sion and a rare evening's entertainment. In the early years between World Wars I and II, radio was still in its infancy. Like the phonograph and a stack of scratchy records, it was wonderful, but it still was not enough. The movies were a big treat, but the movie house was miles away "in town" — a twice-monthly destination to buy supplies. People craved live entertainment, but most rural families went years without hearing a live orchestra or watching actors on a stage. The concert provided that "live" entertainment. Better still, entertainment that starred their own children.

One of the most challenging tasks that befell a rural prairie schoolteacher every year was presenting some form of pageant or play that somehow ensured every student was given an opportunity to contribute. Nothing — neither costumes, songs, nor clever skits — mattered as much as that single fact. And parents? Parents represented much more than an audience.

The teacher needed help and parents were happy to provide it. Fathers hammered together stages, painted scenery, rigged special lights, and cut down and put up Christmas trees. One of the men was given the honour of playing Santa. Mothers stitched amazingly imaginative costumes: military uniforms, fairy gowns with gossamer wings, and outfits that turned children into Christmas candles. The thrifty and enterprising women fashioned some of the costumes so they could be utilized as "Sunday best" long after the concert.

These same moms then baked cakes, tarts, and other treats and either served them, or packaged them up for the children in homemade bags. Usually, one of the mothers or grandmothers could be counted on to play the piano. Some families who had organs or pianos in their front rooms

Young girls in costume for a Christmas event

invited teacher and students to home-style rehearsals. These cooperative efforts of people living in far-flung farms and homesteads staved off the isolation, the loneliness, the sheer monotonous predictability of seemingly endless winter days and nights.

The Prairie Christmas Concert

"Tell us about your Christmas concerts ..."
So great was the importance of the Christmas concert that the production was specifically referred to in the teachers' contracts. As many teachers realized, their ability to produce a truly special concert could be almost as influential in gaining and retaining employment as their formal education. The yuletide equation appeared to be: well-organized, imaginative program, plus well-disciplined performers equals good teacher. A teacher, therefore, became a combination of playwright, director, composer, and musical conductor — and, in some cases, musician.

The provincial government of Alberta and its educational leaders not only acknowledged the popularity of the concert, but also recognized it as a particularly powerful "teachable moment." By 1936, in its *Programme of Studies for the Elementary School*, the government was offering this guidance to teachers: "It is advisable that the Christmas concert, which is one of the important enterprises of the year, should grow out of schoolwork. Thus, the practicing of music, verse speaking and plays, will be carried on during school hours; for these activities are a legitimate part of school life, having a satisfying culmination in the concert itself."

Teachers obliged by creating plays and pageants that reflected rural history, such as Chinook, Alberta's *In the Days of Grandma and Grandpa*, and 1951's Depression-era saga, *Sod*. They also created plays from stories in readers, such as Manitoba's Hodgson School's *Shoe Maker and the Elves*, and stoked the fires of patriotism with stories and songs about war heroes — Blindloss, Alberta's *Crippled Soldier* and Chinook's 1942 duet, *Big Ben*. The productions provided countless musical opportunities for students. In places like Biggar and Admiral, Saskatchewan, lucky students got the chance to play in school bands and orchestras.

All over the Prairies — in overheated, crowded one-room schoolhouses, and, later, inside cavernous gymnasiums of larger city schools — the Christmas concert was unsurpassed as a social, cultural, educational, and spiritual phenomenon. Despite the squalls of infants, clank and scrape of chairs, flickering lights, forgotten lines, miscued action, and other catastrophes, it was an event that provoked reminiscences — fond memories that often became the stuff of legend.

Dedicated and Talented Teachers

Teachers began planning their Christmas concerts early by "brainstorming" with other teachers at summer conventions and workshops. By the fall, pouring over catalogues, they were making notes in five-cent scribblers about costumes and props. The task of planning the concert was so challenging that teachers who moved from school to school soon learned to take their best props and costumes with them. They read plays, poems, and short stories with a new purpose and saw them in an entirely new light. Would this make a good presentation?

Teachers became masters in the art of motivation. They

knew their students' attentiveness, if not learning, improved when concert practice was promised at the end of the day's lessons. Hilda Adock, who taught at Coronation, Alberta, went one step further. In September, she entered into agreements with her students: rehearsals wouldn't begin unless every student was at a certain place in their textbooks by that crucial time before Christmas.

Teachers often had to cajole, scold, or nag to get good performances out of the kids. But, knowing that parents prized the children's happiness and sense of achievement far more than artistic perfection, they didn't push their charges too hard.

As well as pulling the concert together, teachers had to raise funds. They not only needed money for the production, they were expected to buy supplies to make decorations for the classrooms and treats and gifts for the students. Sometimes, with the help of parents, teachers organized raffles and called on area businesses and service clubs for donations. The lengths some teachers went to in carrying out these duties went down in local history.

In the days leading up to Christmas 1936, teacher Alice Moore had finally collected enough money to buy presents for her students. After the kids had agonized over department store catalogues and made their wish lists, Alice completed the order forms. A certain Monday was the deadline for mailing the order. That Monday night, Alice borrowed a pony and set out, bareback, in sub-zero temperatures, on the

19-kilometre ride to the town of Athabasca, Alberta.

Presumably, she found bareback riding was not to her liking, so she stopped at a farm and asked for a saddle. The farmer kindly gave her one, but was not gallant enough to put it on for her. To her consternation, she found the saddle was far too big for the dainty pony. After getting the oversized saddle on, she set out — a little more comfortably — in the pitch black. How many times she had to stop to re-cinch the saddle is not recorded, but it's safe to say she became very accomplished at the task. Finally, the lights of the town came into view. All she had to do now was cross the frozen Athabasca River.

She tied her pony to some bushes and stood on the riverbank, summoning her courage to walk on the ice. Luckily, there were other travellers crossing the river on foot. After watching one after another get across safely, she finally stepped out onto the frozen expanse and slowly made her way across.

Once on the other side, relieved and happy, she walked into the light and warmth of the post office. She picked up her mail, then tried to send her precious order. To her dismay, she was informed that the post-office was closed for business. She knew the kids wouldn't get their gifts in time for Christmas unless she mailed the order that night. With a sinking heart, she rushed outside, where the darkness hid her tears of "frustration, anger and weariness." Determined not to disappoint the children, she vowed not to give up.

The plucky teacher located the home of a storekeeper she had done business with and asked for his help. Fortunately, he was able to use his influence to bend the post office rules. The order got away in time. Many years later, Alice summed up her adventure: "Santa Claus did come to Big Coulee School that year!" she said with a triumphant smile.

Getting There

While teachers like Alice put so much effort into organizing the concerts, parents had to put considerable effort into getting to the big event. Dorothy Hodgson, wife of a former Perdue, Saskatchewan farmer, remembers the journeys well: "We used to go in the big sleigh, with a team, and my husband would heat rocks to keep our feet warm," she recalls. As many as six Hodgson children would be huddled together under blankets, so the big sleigh — actually a wagon with runners instead of wheels — was the perfect vehicle for them. Unfortunately for Dorothy's husband, he couldn't stay for the performance because there was nowhere to shelter the team of horses. He just had to drop off his family and take the team home again.

Jim Storey, who grew up near Dundurn, just south of Saskatoon, says the dads in his community were more fortunate — his school had a barn. He recalls that the men-folk enjoyed that trip to the barn. There were certain ... advantages. "What you also have to remember about those days,"

Jim says, "is that there were farmers who made home-brew. So there was a little bit of that out there in the barn." Little wonder it would take at least 20 minutes before everyone was gathered in the schoolroom-turned-theatre.

Although the sleigh was useful for big families, the most common mode of winter transportation was the cutter. This vehicle was simply a wooden platform placed on runners, with a small shelter built on the platform. The structure, which looked very much like an outhouse, sported a stovepipe that rose through the roof from a small heating appliance.

Controlling the horses from inside the cutter's warm little "house" was easy because reins were fed through a small slot beneath the front window. The driver stood by the window and had an unobstructed view of the team and the road. Farmers knew the landscape well, so didn't often get lost on the snow-covered trails. However, during snowstorms, they relied on their horses to find the way home.

In addition to kids, food, and perhaps presents, parents also carried coal-oil lamps or — if they could afford such luxuries — gas lanterns to the concert in the cutter. There was no power in rural areas during the 1930s and 40s, so they took their own lamps to illuminate the schoolhouse.

Anything That Can Go Wrong...
The weeks and days leading up to the big show were always tense. Often, at the very last moment, catastrophe struck.

Students and teachers, in true "show biz" tradition, redoubled their efforts. Such was the case in Drumheller, Alberta, the afternoon before the Christmas concert of 1934.

The school's lights were flicked off, and the door securely locked. Teacher and students had every reason to feel a sense of satisfaction as they headed home from school that December afternoon. The decorations were terrific and the play was great. All they had to do now was run through the dress rehearsal the next day, and then it would be "Show Time."

The next morning when they opened the door to the school, they stood in stunned dismay: the potbellied stove had belched smoke all night long. The once-white walls were black. The windows were completely blanked out. The big, bright silver bell positioned in the centre of the ceiling — the focal point — was a dull, dirty brown. The would-be thespians became a desperate cleaning crew as teacher and students frantically scrubbed, wiped, and polished as best they could. There was no dress rehearsal, but the show went on as planned!

Another Christmas concert was almost derailed in Vauxhall, Alberta, in 1947. Not by soot, but by snow. Students and teacher woke on the morning of the big show to find that nature had "upstaged" them with one of the biggest blizzards of the season.

Ploughing their way to school and up the steps was one thing — having to plough their way to the desks was another!

Part of the roof had collapsed under the snow's weight and everything — table and desktops, decorations, and even the stovepipe — was buried. Snow removal took precedence over the final rehearsal, but students hit the stage on time that night.

A third story about how young Albertans rose to the occasion comes from Hanna. The class of 1939 was small; only 18 students sat behind the classroom's desks. But this was more than enough to put on what promised to be a wonderful Christmas concert. Then, in the final days before the show, students began waking up with spots. Chicken pox had come to town.

By the eve of the big day, the already-modest enrolment was reduced by 12. Should the concert be cancelled? Not a chance! Six children soldiered on and gave a shorter — but courageous — performance.

These three concerts were all memorable — and successful. But other concerts that delighted audiences, the ones remembered a century later, were those where the unexpected and unpredictable reigned supreme.

Consider the poor teacher in Fiske, Saskatchewan, who inadvertently provided an insightful and hilarious "shadow" drama throughout the concert. Although "hidden" behind a sheet, light from an unwisely positioned lantern made her frantic actions visible to the audience. The cajoling, threatening, exasperated director easily upstaged her young charges that night.

Pity the one frantically scratching youngster in Red Deer, Alberta, who discovered, to his mortification — and his parents' disbelief — that he had an allergic reaction to tension and excitement. The malady remained undiscovered until he twitched onto the stage.

Take a moment to puzzle at the 1926 concert in Craigmyle, Alberta, where a mysterious ailment struck down players in the middle of the performance! So determined were the youngsters that, in spite of their wooziness, they tried to go on with the show. But, after a third young performer collapsed onstage, moms and dads in the audience became alarmed. Attending school trustees wanted the show stopped. The teacher adamantly refused. However, the concert soon ground to a halt as child after child was bundled up in the sleigh and driven home by worried parents. Thankfully, all the children had recovered by the next morning, and the source of the contagion was discovered. A new electric light generator had recently been installed. Unfortunately, no one had thought to make a vent. So the generator that should have enhanced the performance by casting light on the players, felled them by spewing its carbon monoxide exhaust directly under the stage.

Jim Storey, of Dundurn fame, has another tale to share about Christmas concerts. This one involved a truly spectacular show. A few days before Christmas some time in the 1930s, the Storey family set off to see Jim's sister perform at her school, about two and a half miles away. During the

Christmas in the Prairies

concert, someone went outside, perhaps for a trip to the outhouse, perhaps to check the horses. Within minutes, he dashed back inside and spread the word: somebody's house was on fire! It turned out to be the Storeys' place.

By the time the family and most of the concert-goers arrived at the farm, the flaming wreckage of the house had fallen into the cellar. Jim's dad was mortified. He knew only too well what had happened. In the frantic last minutes before they set out for the concert, he had filled the small stove with coal, but neglected to do one small, crucial task.

"What you had to do was burn the gas off with the draughts open," Jim explains. "I guess they were in a hurry to get to the school. He shut down the draughts instead of leaving them open." The gas inside built up to a critical level and then, "the stove just exploded."

The farm Jim's parents worked on was actually owned by the operator of the lumberyard in the nearby town of Hanley, so the operator quickly moved a ready-made house to the same location and put it over the same cellar. Much to the Storeys' delight, they had a roof over their heads that Christmas, after all.

This next story took place "somewhere in southern Saskatchewan, sometime in the 1900s." Small town citizens are, as a rule, not quite as quick to change the prevailing mores as the folks in big cities. However, they are far more likely to notice these changes in mores — and to talk about them — as one discomfited teacher discovered.

46

The Prairie Christmas Concert

The young teacher, Sarah Scott, unwisely decided to use the school Christmas concert to answer her detractors. She wrote a song, creatively skewering the gossips, then coached the kids to perform it. Imagine the shocked silence when parents heard their own children sing the following ditty:

Merry Christmas Mrs. Jonathan, Merry Christmas!
Mrs. Rip Van Winkle's sharp tongue made her
Husband blue,
But Dame Winkle had nothing on you.
Merry Christmas, Mrs. Jonathan, Merry Christmas!

Merry Christmas, Mrs. Brown, Merry Christmas!
Everyone knows where you go night after night,
Do you think at your age it is right?
Merry Christmas Mrs. Brown, Merry Christmas!

There were other verses — many others. The teacher's number-one target happened to be the person behind the curtain accompanying the students on the piano. Someone, most likely one of the conscience-stricken children, had tipped her off before the performance. To the teacher's sudden consternation, the vengeful accompanist kept playing at the end of the teacher's song, and the kids kept singing:

Merry Christmas, Miss Sarah Scott, Merry Christmas!
Wearing short dresses to flash your lacy pink panties,

Tells us your lifestyle is full of frailties.
Merry Christmas, Miss Sarah Scott, Merry Christmas!

The applause was thunderous.

The Essence of the Prairies

As time marched on, the one-room school passed into history, and Christmas concerts were performed in gymnasiums and community halls in villages, towns, and cities. Today, the props are grander, the programmes more sophisticated, and the casts much bigger. But some things will never change. In those frantic few seconds before the curtain goes up, students feel the same excitement and terror their parents and grandparents felt. And they ask themselves the same dreadful questions: What if I forget my lines, or the lyrics, or the moves?

Many of the kids who stood trembling on the makeshift stages of the one-room schools are now sitting on the other side of the curtain, watching their grandchildren perform. A glimpse at the 1994 Christmas pageant in Banff, Alberta, proves that the tradition of community Yuletide entertainment is still going strong.

In the large Eric Harvie Theatre, the master of ceremonies led more than 1000 pageant-goers in Christmas song. The festive mood set, it was "on with the show!"

And what a show it was: youthful ballet dancers from a local dance studio gave a graceful rendition of *The Nutcracker*;

kids from the day-care centre provided spirited recitations; and troops of students from the elementary school performed well-timed routines. With a wave of a magic wand, a tall, glittering Christmas tree magically appeared. And in a climactic surprise act, the school staff — dressed as woodland animals, a clown, and a winged angel — trooped on the stage and burst into seasonal song.

Maja Geber, who had been the concert co-ordinator during the 1980s, says the pageant was really the only event that brought everyone in the busy community together every year. In recounting the event's significance to the community, Geber noted that the concert had been a tradition in the town since the 1950s.

None of the youthful performers in the theatre that year, or the years since, knew how the tradition of the school Christmas concert had begun. And few will ever realize the significant role it has played in the social, cultural, and spiritual lives of prairie residents.

Chapter 3
The Christmas Tree

hether it is lifted from a cardboard box or taken home from a shopping mall parking lot, today's prairie residents tend to take their Christmas tree for granted. Christmas without a tree is almost unthinkable, but scarcely three generations ago, the reverse was true. As recently as the early 1940s, a farm family that had a Christmas tree and placed presents beneath it was actually celebrating more than Christmas. That fortunate family was celebrating its ability to afford those traditional symbols of the season.

The First Christmas Tree of the Prairies
Somehow, with grit, determination, and stoicism, the Red River colony, the Canadian West's first agricultural settle-

ment, had survived it all: scurvy, animosity between Irish and Scottish factions, near starvation, and warfare between the Hudson's Bay Company and the North-West Company. In 1862, 50 years after the first colonists had set up camp on the banks of the Red River (near present-day Winnipeg) much had changed. And that year, at Christmas, there was another change in store.

Alexander Grant Dallas, the new governor of Rupert's Land, had arrived in the colony to oversee the immense 1.5 million square mile Hudson's Bay Company land grant that extended to the Rockies. Dallas did not come to Red River alone. He brought his wife, Jane. Faced with the task of making her drab surroundings more festive for Christmas entertaining, Jane was saddened to realize that the colony had never had a Christmas tree. As the daughter of Sir James Douglas (the governor of the colony of Vancouver Island), Jane's childhood Christmases in and around Fort Victoria undoubtedly included Christmas trees. She set to work with a will.

Finding a tree was not a problem for Red River settlers, but decorating it in suitable fashion was another matter. At that time, ingenuity and handicraft skill substituted for packaged ornaments. Jane and her friends carved hearts and stars from cakes of yellow soap, and made garlands from beads and berries. But Jane also wanted something shiny to put on her tree, so she scavenged foil lining from empty boxes at the Fort Garry store. Still not satisfied, she commissioned the fort's tinsmith to make small candleholders and then cut regular candles down to fit them.

Then she turned her attention to gifts. After all, what would Christmas be without toys for the children? For miles downriver, shops were scoured for playthings. Jane and her assistants scrounged a few dolls and Noah's arks and added them to the homemade gifts arrayed in and around the first Christmas tree of the Prairies.

Christmas Trees as Big Business

One of the first entrepreneurs to turn Christmas trees into cash — certainly the first in Calgary — was a Sarcee man named Brave Foxtail. In the early 1900s, plenty of small spruce trees grew on the Sarcee reserve lands near Calgary. Foxtail knew that city people wanted these trees at Christmastime. He and other band members also wanted something at this time of year: funds for the December 26 communal celebrations on the reserve.

Foxtail, soon christened "The Christmas Tree King," came up with a way to please everyone. The Sarcee men set to work. They felled the trees, took them to the city, and sold them to the city folk. As Foxtail predicted, this raised enough funds for their own Christmas celebrations.

Brave Foxtail lived to the ripe old age of 91 — long enough to see Calgary's Sarcee Christmas tree trade grow far bigger than his original vision. Every December, horse-drawn sleighs full of evergreens slipped slowly down the snow-covered streets and avenues of the city's residential neighbourhoods. As they went from house to house, band members didn't have to press people to buy the fragrant trees.

After answering the door and peeking past a smiling band member, sons, daughters, or parents would duck back inside and announce excitedly that the Christmas trees had arrived. There was a scurry to the front windows. Dad or Mom would reach for some cash, put on a coat, slip into boots, and tromp down the wooden front steps. There, in the cold early evening or Saturday afternoon, a careful curbside inspection took place. Meanwhile, a patient horse snorted clouds of white vapour into the air while waiting for each family to lighten the sleigh's load.

Brave Foxtail's descendants carried on the profitable business until the mid-1930s, when other entrepreneurs realized there was a profit to be made in Christmas trees. Farmers began selling trees wholesale to other growers and suppliers. In this era of the automobile, it was far more cost effective for growers and suppliers to set up shop in a vacant lot, or make a deal with a service station, than to painstakingly take their wares from door to door.

"Business no good ... too many trees in Calgary; so many they not half sold," Chief Joe Big Plume complained to the *Calgary Herald* in 1936. Unable to compete, the Sarcee Christmas tree merchants gradually gave up their seasonal trade, and Calgary's unique door-to-door Christmas tree business became a memory.

The "Reasonable Facsimile" Trees

During the first 30 years of the 1900s, few prairie families had Christmas trees in their living rooms at Christmastime; at least, not Christmas trees we would recognize today. The first reason was that, on the bald prairie, there were no evergreen forests where settlers could take their hatchets and help themselves. The second reason was the ever-present lack of money.

Nobody was more surprised at this woeful state of affairs than the thousands of immigrants who stepped off the boats and trains to make their new homes on the Canadian Prairies.

"Oh, it was the land of milk and honey," says Dorothy Hodgson with a laugh, while recounting her own 30-odd years of meagre Christmases. Immigrant farmers soon discovered that a parcel of 160 acres wasn't enough to keep a family going. "Although they didn't know it at the time," Dorothy adds. "These young boys, coming from England didn't know anything about farming. My own brothers didn't know anything about farming. They said they farmed, but they didn't really ... My husband was another one. He was not interested in farming. He had more of an engineering mind. He could have done very, very well in engineering."

Not one of Dorothy's neighbours was the ideal farmer envisioned by Clifford Sifton when he launched his marketing campaign to fill the West. Instead, these were Birmingham machinists, Glasgow shipwrights, and derby-hatted London office workers. The failure rate, something that is not talked about much today, was enormous. Thousands of acres of the free land were simply abandoned. "Have given up the unequal task. Help Yourself." was one note left nailed to an empty two-room house. Hundreds of rotting, tumbled-down shacks and farmhouses dotted the Prairies, mute testimony to naivety, inability, and the unforgiving land itself.

In these hard times, having any extra money to spend on a Christmas tree was unthinkable. Even today, Dorothy, who is over 100 years old, scoffs at the idea. However, that didn't mean her family went without something festive to put in the corner of the large area that served as kitchen, dining room, and living room: "We cut little poplar saplings and we made paper chains — coloured paper; pages of the Eaton's catalogue — and we had little candles — I don't know why we didn't burn the house down. That was our decoration."

While Dorothy and her family were making paper chains, other farming families in the neighbouring province of Alberta were doing what they could to bring some Christmas cheer into their homes. In the small settlement of Brooks, south of Calgary, two young men, J.A. Hawkinson and Carl Anderson, went Christmas shopping after delivering their loads of wheat.

Hawkinson had a wife and kids at home, and he knew that a Christmas tree would mean a lot. Back in Minnesota, where the family had emigrated from, there were evergreens everywhere. But not here! The two stores in Brooks had none, and he was getting frustrated. Desperate for a tree, or at least to voice his complaint, Hawkinson went to the only symbol of authority in the tiny hamlet of 200: the CPR station. But there was no help to be had there, either.

It was too far to travel back to their farm that night, so the men stayed in Brooks. The next morning, they got up early, harnessed the horses and set out for home. It was bitterly cold, so the men chose to walk beside their wagon, simply to keep warm. For the family man, it was a depressing journey. He knew his family would be disappointed at his failure to find a Christmas tree. Finally tiring, Hawkinson jumped up on the wagon, and just as quickly jumped to the ground again in shock and surprise.

"Why'dja do it?" he yelled happily to his friend. Anderson, bewildered, demanded to know what Hawkinson was talking about. Getting no answer other than a beaming smile, Anderson jumped up onto the wagon and looked inside. There, at the bottom, was a beautiful spruce tree. It probably took a while for him to convince his happy friend that he hadn't put the tree in the wagon.

As soon as the men got home, Hawkinson proudly showed his family the beautiful tree. Much to his surprise, they were not thrilled. While he and his friend had been away, the kids had carried home a tumbleweed, placed it in the corner of their two-room cabin and decorated it with Christmas ornaments they had brought all the way from Minnesota. To them, the tumbleweed was a real Christmas tree!

The Christmas Tree

Despite his family's surprising reaction, Hawkinson still treasured his tree and wondered who had put it the wagon. Years later, he discovered the "secret Santa" was CPR district engineer Augustus Griffin. After listening to the young father's lament, he had gone out and cut down one of the hundreds of trees he had planted for the CPR and had placed it in the wagon.

June and Bob's Tree

In the same era, when cities were small and friendly, June Cox and her brother, Bob, were sent to buy the family's Christmas tree — even though they were "only kids."

"We went to a service station about five blocks from where we lived," June recalls. Once there, the kids were faced with a large choice of trees. It didn't bother them in the least. "We knew the space we had to put it in. We had a den with a fireplace, and a radio — we listened to the hockey games on Saturday — and the tree would be in the far corner. We bought the tree — twenty-five cents or fifty cents probably — and we tied our tree to the toboggan and started back home."

One year, on the way home, they saw a group of kids playing on a slope. "They were all sliding and having fun," says June. "They were using old pieces of cardboard — that's what you did, you know, if you didn't have a toboggan. We had one, but our tree was on it."

Being responsible youngsters, they didn't risk taking the tree off the toboggan. They simply grabbed a piece of cardboard and took off. When the light began to fade, the rosy-cheeked children collected their toboggan with its Christmas-tree cargo and started for home again.

This simple Christmas event had no dramatic ending. The kids didn't lose the tree. Their mother didn't scold them for taking so long. And it never occurred to June or Bob that the afternoon would ever be significant to them. However, when June relates this and other stories to today's vigilant parents, they are surprised that June's mother allowed such young children to go so far on their own. They are also amazed that the two children were entrusted with the task of choosing the tree and bringing it home.

June feels that by being entrusted with such tasks, she and Bob learned self-reliance and decision-making, and had fun learning it. Many people of June's generation feel sorry for today's youngsters because they don't have the kind of freedom that was possible in their own youth. They suspect today's children will never feel that their Christmas trees are truly their own in the way that June and Bob did when their tree went up in the corner of the den.

A Simply Beautiful Christmas

By the mid-1950s, trekking into the woods to chop down your own Christmas tree was, for most people, merely a fond memory. However, things were different in Grey Campbell's household.

Campbell, a retired Alberta RCMP officer, had made the

decision to take up ranching. He moved to the C7 Ranch in the foothills of Alberta's Rocky Mountains. For 12 years, the Campbell family — Grey, his wife Eleanor, and their four children — lived in relative isolation, 90 kilometres from any large store and 30 kilometres from the nearest village. Far from feeling disadvantaged, the family loved the isolation. That was the sheer beauty of it! Life was simple, clean, and uncomplicated.

"We made a ceremony out of everything," Grey recalled when writing about his ranching experiences years later. And that included getting the Christmas tree. Living so far away from civilization, the Campbell family couldn't buy one from a city parking lot. And they wouldn't have done so, even if they could.

"Getting our tree was a very special occasion," Grey wrote. "And that meant team and sleigh." After harnessing the horses, the family set out in the crisp, cool breeze. Their horses, Prince and Brownie, plodded through the snow to the top of the ridge and climbed up the valley through the Campbells' herd of Herefords. The sight of the rancher and his family meant only one thing to the cattle: extra feed! Within a few seconds, cows were plodding along, too, following the sleigh at a respectable distance at the rear. Laughing and clowning, son Dane, who was snug in his own sleigh tied to the larger one, waved the cattle away. Once the horses had climbed up the gentle slopes of the valley, Campbell tethered them out of the wind, and the family set off into the trees.

The kids inspected each tree closely. After careful

deliberation, family members took a vote and chose their tree. The boys ran through the snow to the sleigh for the axe and saw. The fir came down within a few minutes, and Grey dragged it to the waiting sleighs.

At the memory of their first year on the ranch and that first Christmas tree, Grey Campbell echoed the age-old familiar prairie refrain: "There was little enough money and nothing for frills," he wrote. They decorated the tree with whatever they could find: "... some strands of tarnished tinsel Eleanor found among our effects, which had been stored throughout the war. She added color and a measure of enchantment by hanging toys and rattles."

Inspired by the novelty of the Christmas tree, Dane threw on his coat and gloves and raced outside. Soon, he was busy collecting small boughs that had been trimmed off the tree. Crouching down in the snow in front of the house, he painstakingly tied bits of fat and peanuts onto the miniature limbs. The clever result: a Christmas tree birdfeeder.

"I suppose," Grey mused years later, "a city dweller used to elaborate displays in stores, and the lights and shiny balls and tinsel one may purchase would find ours a shabby effort. But the children were satisfied, and that was all that mattered."

Of course, the tree the Campbells put up in their modest ranch house didn't have to be elegant to bring them pleasure. It gave them an opportunity to have fun as a family. The Christmas tree meant fond memories in the making; memories of family love.

Chapter 4
Santa and His Helpers

Santa, as every kid knows, can't be everywhere at once. So, he has helpers. These Santa-stand-ins come from all walks of life and travel all over the place. You just never know where you'll find a great Santa. He — or she — could be anywhere: at a school concert, in a Doukhobor village, or hiding in somebody's imagination.

An Interview with Santa

In 1982, Myrna Morris was working as a reporter for a newspaper in Fort Qu'Appelle, Saskatchewan. A few weeks before Christmas, she was given an assignment to write a feature story based on an interview with Santa Claus.

Myrna remembered how strongly she had believed in

Santa when she was a little girl. But she was no longer a child. She was an adult reporter covering important local stories. When she told her friends about this assignment, she suffered some good-natured ribbing. After that, she judiciously decided she wouldn't tell anyone else. As she began thinking about how she would handle the story, she heard a booming voice, "Hello, Little One!" Her "interview" with the Jolly Old Elf was about to begin.

"I knew Santa Claus would have a booming voice!" she wrote in the story that appeared in the *Fort Qu'Appelle Times* three days before Christmas Day that year. "He looked me square in the eyes and said, 'The reason I chose you to visit me, Little One, is because I have a message for you to take back to everyone' So that was it," Myrna concluded, "I had been chosen.

"'Here is my message,' he continued, tugging thoughtfully on his snow-white beard and settling his glasses comfortably on his nose. 'It has come to my attention that some folks are losing their enthusiasm for the Christmas season,' he stated. 'They worry that it is being too commercialized, and that it may someday lose all of its meaning and importance. But you know, Little One, that will never happen, as long as you all remember to do one thing; and that is to see Christmas through the eyes of the children,' said Santa.

"'As long as there are little ones who put on school Christmas concerts, who write me letters each year, who set out their stockings on Christmas Eve, who leave me snacks and listen carefully for my reindeer on the roof until they fall asleep, Christmas will never lose its magic. That is why I was created,' said Santa, 'to make sure that the spirit of Christmas can be kept alive through children's belief in me, in good times and bad.

"'So tell everyone,' Santa instructed me, 'not to feel discouraged. I know it must be difficult at times, with Santas on every street corner, and the monetary value that has been attached to having a good Christmas. I know there are poor people and lonely people who despair at Christmas, and evil people, who use Christmas for themselves. But above all else, there are still the children. They don't see the greed, the evil or the commercialization of the season. They only feel the spirit of love and giving that is the spirit of Santa Claus. It is there,' he assured me, 'I see it every year, in their trusting faces, and read it in their letters to me.

"'So you see, Little One,' concluded Santa, 'as long as we have children and a Santa Claus we will still have the spirit of Christmas. And I intend to be around for a long, long time,' he chuckled."

Outstanding Stand-ins

John Wilson, a transplanted British newspaperman, was looking forward to Christmas 1908 — his second festive season on a farm near Prince Albert, Saskatchewan. It wasn't because the food would be better, and it wasn't because he was expecting expensive gifts. It was because some single women had moved to town! This fact brightened the lives of Prince Albert's bachelors considerably.

That Christmas Eve, John and his friends joined the high-spirited girls in a special sleigh ride. One of the young women was very dressed up and adjusted her festive garments as they reached their destination — a nearby Doukhobor village. Once there, the girls eagerly set about their Christmas Eve task of visiting each of the homes and leaving toys for the children. The one girl's finery impressed the village children. She was dressed as Santa Claus, beard and all, and the others were her elves!

In another area of Saskatchewan, a quarter of a century later, Jim Storey saw a special Santa — his first — at a school concert. The concert was pretty much the only place rural kids saw Santa's helpers in those days. It was not until after World War II that Santa-suited men appeared in department stores or stood on street corners in aid of charity. Street corners were few and far between in rural Saskatchewan, and the closest most people got to a department store was browsing through the Eaton's catalogue.

Jim remembers that the gas and coal oil lamps people had brought into the school had given the room a warm, somewhat mysterious glow. He was looking at the shadows the lamps were throwing here and there, when in came Santa Claus with a booming "Ho Ho Ho!"

"He scared me right out of my mind!" Jim laughs, the memory still fresh 70 years later. It's a good bet that young

Santa and His Helpers

Jim wouldn't have been worried had he realized it was his own father under the beard and red hat.

Every once in a long time, though, a very special pseudo-Santa emerges. One of the best remembered in rural Alberta was a travelling salesman who worked for Love Feeds Limited. His name was Jack Fulton. He was built a lot like Santa, and his voice, reportedly, boomed just the way Santa's should. He was very friendly, laughed a lot, and loved the kids. Legend has it that, in the month of December, Jack had more than seed catalogues and samples in the trunk of his car. He had an entire Santa Claus suit tucked away in there, too. Nowhere was a man who was prepared.

One December while in Drumheller, Jack was invited to dinner by a farm family on the very evening of the school Christmas concert. It was all the three daughters in the household could do to eat their supper. They were performing that night, so excitement was running high. The family invited him to the concert, but Jack declined, saying he couldn't be in the audience because he had another appointment to keep.

He didn't actually fib. Jack really wasn't going to be in the audience — he was going to be on the stage. His "appointment" was to play Santa Claus at the concert. He made his way to the school, quickly changed into his costume, and made his grand entrance. Did he worry that the girls would recognize him? If so, he needn't have. They were as delighted as their other classmates when the Jolly Old Elf marched onto the stage. They had no idea that this was the same man who had sat across the dinner table from them three hours earlier.

In another part of the province, some years before Jack was doing his rounds as Santa, Jeane Jervais, a teacher at Sedalia, was having trouble finding anyone to play the part at her Christmas concert. She told her fiancé, John McLeod, about her problem. John said he could convince a friend of his to play the part. Jeane must have been dubious: John worked in Calgary, more than 300 kilometres away. What friend would travel that distance in the middle of winter to play Santa?

The big night came, and — much to Jeane's relief — so did Santa. Not just any old Santa, either; this Santa was terrific! He charmed the children; therefore, he also charmed their parents. Jeane was pleased, but her delight turned to shock as she discovered that under that red hat and behind that white beard was her fiancé, John!

Happily, most Christmas concerts were held at night, which meant that organizers could use the cover of darkness outside to enhance the reality of Santa's arrival. One Cotswold, Alberta, school-board-trustee-turned-Santa would race around the schoolhouse shouting, "Whoa there, Prancer, Whoa, there Vixen!" at the top of his lungs, while an accomplice made scraping sounds outside, high on the school wall. There could be no doubt about it, you could actually hear those reindeer pulling Santa's sleigh right onto the roof! All eyes flew up to the trapdoor in the ceiling. Sure enough, the

trap door opened and, with considerable huffing and puff-
ing — the trap-door entrance was a tight squeeze — down
came Santa!

A Santa Sighting

One Christmas Eve in the late 1950s, Edmonton radio morn-
ing-show host John Barton was driving home with his wife
Lesley, and their children, Juley (seven) and Reid (five), after
visiting an aunt and uncle. John remembers that trip clearly:

"It was after dark, and we had to hurry home because
Santa was on his way. The kids were in the back seat, punch-
ing each other." John laughs and corrects himself. "No, they
were excited all right, but behaving themselves. After all this
was the night of nights! They just wanted us to hurry home,
hurry home! We were maybe ten blocks from the Edmonton
Municipal Airport, and it was pitch black outside. Lesley
looked up and spotted something in the sky. What she had
seen, of course, was simply the blinking red light of an air-
plane coming in for a landing. 'Oh look!' she said."

John had seen the light at the same time. Before Lesley
had a chance to give the game away, he turned to the kids
and said, "Do you see what I see?" The children stopped their
excited babble and silently leaned forward, their eyes following their father's outstretched arm.

John then said, "If you're very careful, if you look hard,
directly ahead and up into the sky ... what do you see? Do you
see something that looks like a nose?" Both kids looked hard

and said, "Oh, my gosh!"

"They couldn't believe it," says John, smiling at the memory. "Their jaws just dropped and they just stared!"

The right time, the right place, and the power of suggestion was all it took. To Juley and Reid Barton, there was no doubt. It just had to be Rudolph leading Santa's team of reindeer! Now the kids were really in a panic to get home. John had a ready answer that calmed them down: "I said, 'You don't have to worry too much, because Santa's working that end of town right now.'"

Leslie rolled her eyes at her husband's slick act. "I just thought it was a hoot," John recalls with a laugh.

Chapter 5
Special Gifts

I n most homes today, gifts are piled high under the Christmas tree and long, fat Christmas stockings hang heavily above the fireplace. But scarcely two generations ago, the Christmas morning scene was quite different. Gifts were few. And compared to today's expensive items, they seem meagre, indeed. The reason is simple. Any time before the 1950s, most Prairie people suffered deprivation 12 months of the year — Christmas included. Perhaps that's why the few small gifts opened on Christmas morning were valued far more than most of the gifts we give or receive today.

Gifts From The Heart
During the 1930s, many gifts were handmade. As Christmas

approached, the clever craftsmanship of thousands of creative mothers and fathers became a meaningful and especially heartfelt way to compensate for a lack of cash. This was certainly the way it was at the Storeys' place just south of Saskatoon.

"We had nothing. Most people had nothing," says Jim Storey. "But you know, we were actually better off than the town people. We had gardens and animals," he adds, voicing the typical hard-times sentiment.

What Jim and his sisters also had were creative, caring parents. When the Storeys couldn't afford to buy gifts, they made them. One Christmas, Jim's dad made him a wooden horse, brightly painted, with real horsehair for the mane and tail.

"That was the highlight of my life," says Jim. "He made it out in the horse barn. That's where he hid it, you see, so I never knew."

Another gift made an impression: a "store-bought" toy. "Later on, I got a dump-truck that had actual lights on it; lights that really worked!" To young Jim, this gift was magic. As the years passed, the gift became even more amazing to Jim because he realized his parents couldn't have afforded it. "My dad must have really scrambled to buy it. I'm sure my mother and dad went without so we had those kinds of things. But they never talked about it."

Neighbourly Generosity

In years gone by, some of the most memorable Christmas presents children received were given out at the school Christmas concert. Three young girls, daughters of Americans who had recently immigrated to rural Alberta, had been forced to leave behind all their toys in order to make the journey. The girls sorely missed those toys, especially their dolls.

While attending the Christmas concert at their new school in Cayley, Dorothy, Leola, and Cleo Houghton saw their first evergreen Christmas tree. When they looked more closely, they saw much more than that! The Christmas tree boughs drooped with the weight of presents. Tucked into some of those branches were wonderful dolls.

Not long after Santa arrived and began pulling presents from the tree and announcing names of lucky children, Cleo felt her mother nudging her. Santa had called her name! Then, Santa was calling her sisters' names, too. All three received beautiful new dolls. Not homemade dolls, like the ones their mother had made early in the summer, but real dolls! Years later, the girls learned that the schoolhouse Santa was actually an intermediary for an anonymous gift-giver — their neighbour, a generous woman who had befriended their mother.

The Lost Gift

In the Logan household in Calgary, late on Christmas Eve 1933, Lila Logan surveyed her living room to make sure

A prairie Christmas greeting

everything was ready for the next morning. While checking the gifts under the tree, the mother of seven experienced a sudden pang of remorse. Somehow, it seemed that little Ila wouldn't have quite as much to open the following morning as the other kids. The stores had long since closed. But she had to do something. She went to her husband and they came up with a solution.

Special Gifts

Reluctantly, Jim Logan pulled out a two-dollar bill from his wallet. He didn't begrudge his little girl the extra gift, but two dollars was a lot of money in those days. A nickel bought a chocolate bar, a dime got you into a movie, and 50 cents filled the car's gas tank. Too proud to go on relief, Jim had accepted a minimum-wage job for the City of Calgary. Ironically, he was a clerk in the department responsible for handing out welfare cheques. With seven children to feed, he could have earned more money as a relief recipient than his job paid.

That precious two-dollar bill was slipped into a crisp white envelope. The envelope was hidden away in the branches of the Christmas tree — one more present for Ila.

Christmas morning! After all the laughter, the cries of delight, the happy confusion of torn wrapping paper and swiftly emptied boxes, came the burning question: Ila, what will you buy with your two dollars? Only a blank stare in return. What two dollars?

Lila's face went white. It was difficult enough to part with an additional two dollars, but now, to lose it? Surely not. The hunt was on.

And hunt they did, going belly-to-the-floor to peer under the couch and chairs. They searched all over the house and then went into the backyard, where the discarded wrapping paper and boxes had been deposited. The wrappings were brought back in and strewn over the floor again. Hands flew this way and that in this desperate Christmas

Day quest, anxious eyes scanning the refuse for the elusive white envelope.

That envelope was never found. The saga of the missing gift became an oft-repeated story at get-togethers with friends and neighbours well into the New Year.

Santa Outdone

The following year, as Christmas approached, the Logans were determined that Ila would have a doll from Santa. Mr. Claus must have agreed. Under the Christmas tree on that next exciting Christmas morning was a big, bright, beautiful doll. But due to an unusual event in Ontario, there was more — much more!

In May of that year, in a rural Ontario hamlet, an astonishing biological miracle had occurred. Inside a log farmhouse, Elzire Dionne had given birth to five tiny babies; living, breathing quintuplets! The phenomenon known as "the Dionne Quints" sparked the wonder of people all over the globe. Some of those people were in business, and business was booming. The quints were featured on fans, plates, spoons, pens, books, and t-shirts, as well as in newsreels and documentary films. Most of all, there were dolls, tens of thousands of them. Singly and in sets of five, the quint dolls were worth millions to their makers.

Just as the real babies fascinated adults, the doll babies captured the imaginations of little girls everywhere. The first sets of quint dolls made their very timely and profitable appearance in the gift-giving weeks just before Christmas. They became the hottest toy on the market, outselling even the Shirley Temple doll. Among the captivated in Calgary were young Ila Logan and her sisters. The girls would press their noses against the windows of McGill's Drugs. There, on the other side of the pane, in all their cuddlesome baby-doll glory, were the quints, snuggled into their own little wooden bed. Price: $4.95. However, if you were a loyal McGill customer, the dolls could be yours, absolutely free.

As a shopping incentive, McGill's offered customers points for cash register tapes. The shopper with the highest number of points would win those dolls.

"Poor little Ila," friends and neighbours must have thought, as they remembered the lost two-dollar bill of the previous Christmas. "Poor little Ila," they thought again, as they scribbled her name on their drug-store receipts.

Weeks later, waiting for Ila under the Logans' tree on Christmas morning, was not one, not two, not even five dolls, but six! That lost envelope, McGill's Drugs, and the miracle in North Bay had unwittingly conspired to outdo even Santa Claus. Ila was beaming. This particular gift from her family and friends was too big to lose!

Present In the Snow

Gertie Minor fell in love and, at the tender age of 18, married her sweetheart, John. As was not uncommon in the 1940s, the couple lived with the groom's family on their prosperous

Sand Hill, Saskatchewan, ranch. Gertie tried to settle in, but the adjustment wasn't easy. She wasn't accustomed to a place where the women slipped a haunch of beef into the oven at 3 a.m. so it would be ready to feed 50 hungry men. Everything about the family and the ranch — all 50,000 sprawling acres of it — was new, bewildering, exhausting, and intimidating, including her energetic, tough-as-nails father-in-law, "Pop" Minor.

Like father, like son — at least behind the wheel. After all, it was Pop who had taught his son how to drive, which meant fast. "Pass that son-of-a-bitch!" was Pop's top of his lungs advice when son John was driving, no matter how fast they were bouncing along the back roads.

Some time in December, John secretly chose a present for his new wife. A few days before Christmas, he went off to town to run errands, and to pick up the gift — he hoped. He wasn't sure it would fit in the back of his truck. Luckily, the huge container slid in without any trouble. Eager to get home, as usual, he drove like the wind along the slippery, winding back roads. Speeding around a sharp corner, the additional weight in the back slew the truck around. The container in the truck bed broke loose and went flying off the pickup and into the snow-covered underbrush seven metres from the road.

John skidded to a halt, backed up the truck, and got out to have a look. He couldn't believe it: the crate had broken open and the gift was completely exposed. There, in the bushes, just waiting for someone to tickle its ivories, was Gertie's brand new piano — without a scratch on it.

John jumped back into the truck and sped home in order to get something to pick the piano up. Rushing into the house, he shouted for Gertie, telling her he needed her help with a sick cow. As she grabbed her coat and ran out the door behind John, she must have wondered about the unpleasant task she was getting herself into. Men in the yard had already hitched a team to a stoneboat, a rough sled used to haul manure. John leapt into the stoneboat with the men, and Gertie followed right behind in the truck.

When they got to the site, Gertie was stunned to discover that the "sick cow" was actually her Christmas present. There it was, just sitting there, waiting to be played. The sight was so outrageous that they all collapsed with laughter. Gertie waded through thigh-high snow and began to bang out Christmas carols right then and there.

Christmas Shopping in September

Dorothy Hodgson arrived in Saskatchewan soon after World War I. She married, had six children, and she and her farmer husband struggled to make ends meet. Compared to their earlier Depression-era deprivations, the Hodgson fortunes had improved somewhat by the 1940s. As the family had grown, so, too, had the original cramped two-room farmhouse the newlyweds had first moved into. The family revelled in its newly expanded four-room, 767-square-foot home, which, like so many others, still had no electricity or indoor plumbing.

With her husband in uniform and away from home, Dorothy spent the wartime years as a single mother. Everyone missed Dad. However, with the arrival of a soldier's pay and 13-year-old Audrey's 25-cents-an-hour baby-sitting money, poverty's leering spectre no longer stared them in the face. But there were plenty of reminders that its cruel presence hovered not far away. Despite lack of money, Christmases were eagerly anticipated and painstakingly planned.

In the weeks leading up to December 25, the coal-lamps burned late into the night at the Hodgson house as Dorothy created her children's gifts. "I remember sitting up at night, sewing little articles for their Christmas presents after they'd gone to bed so they wouldn't see them," Dorothy recalls.

Christmas planning and shopping began months before the festive season. For rural families, there were two ways to "go Christmas shopping." The first was to go all the way to the kitchen table and open up the book that Christmas dreams were made of — the Eaton's Catalogue.

Audrey Rutledge, Dorothy's daughter, remembers the excitement of choosing gifts from the book, and then the nervousness when the order arrived. "Everybody had got a little bit of an order in there, and you wanted to keep everything a secret from the other guys," she says. It was Mom who opened the parcel and very carefully handed out what she knew everyone had ordered for someone else. Audrey remembers some of those gifts. "There would be pencils, a broach would be another gift ... ribbons for someone's hair ... a comb..." As the children grew older, gifts became a little more sophisticated. A fountain pen was a prized gift. "We had ink wells at school," Audrey comments, "so a fountain pen would be a big deal."

Sometimes the choice of gifts brought unexpected reactions. One Christmas, when Dorothy's son Chuck was 8 or 10 years old, he burst into tears during the gift exchange. When Dorothy asked what was wrong, he told her he felt bad because he had spent only 10 cents on her, and 59 cents on his brother Fred. Dorothy comforted the youngster by waving the little dishwashing mop he had given her and telling him it was a terrific gift because she really wanted it.

The other way to shop was to go "to town," which, for the Hodgson family, meant the tiny hamlet of Perdue. Gift buying was done at the general store, "which at that time seemed so big. It had everything from clothing, to hardware, to food, to just about everything."

Out in the country, there was none of the mad Christmas Eve scramble that we experience today. People ordered things weeks, even months, in advance. The catalogue was dog-eared and tattered long before December arrived. After making her list, Dorothy headed "to town" to see Abe Witten, the proprietor of the general store.

"Now, Abe, here's my list from Eaton's catalogue. What can you do?" she would ask him. Abe would look at the list.

"I can do this and this ... and I can do better than this ..."

"He was very, very good to me," says Dorothy. Of course, Dorothy was good to him, too, giving the local merchant the opportunity to beat Eaton's. It wasn't likely Eaton's was going to do anything extra for Dorothy, but Abe Witten would.

"I'll save these things for you, or you can pay me when you like," Abe would say, which usually meant after the harvest was taken in and the crop sold.

"He didn't charge you any interest on that," Dorothy remembers. "And he always gave you a big forty-pound box of apples when you paid your bill."

Then, months before the next holiday season, the cycle of Christmas planning and ordering would begin all over again.

Gifts From "Across The Pond"

Back in Essex, England, Dorothy Hodgson's sister would pack up Christmas parcels for the family and send them to Saskatchewan. "She had one little girl and my first daughter was just about two years younger than she was, so I used to get her hand-me-downs, which were very, very useful," says Dorothy. "She used to send me a few clothes, too, because I couldn't afford to buy anything for myself, either. Also in the parcel, she would have little toys for the children. Little paint boxes, crayons, pencil boxes, little books, too, nursery rhymes and bible stories."

The parcel also contained a seasonal delicacy, which

was actually two gifts in one. "She sent me a round aluminum bowl with a Christmas pudding inside. It had a lid on it with a snap fastener. We used that bowl for years!"

Dorothy was grateful beyond measure. At the time, her sister never really knew how grateful. Personal pride in the face of poverty kept Dorothy Hodgson mute. "I never told her the conditions we were living in," she admitted. "When I went over in '58, for a visit, and I told her some of the things, she said, 'Why didn't you ever tell me?' I said, 'I couldn't.' I just couldn't let her know what conditions were like."

The irony of it, Dorothy points out, was that "After the war, we sent them parcels!"

Giving Back

Hundreds of prairie families had friends and relatives in the U.K. and other European countries. In these war-torn countries, people struggled to shake off the everyday household privations that lingered stubbornly for years after the V.E. Day celebrations.

The Hudson's Bay Company came up with an Overseas Food Parcel Program. It assisted thousands of Canadian families that were eager to share the Dominion's post-war Christmas bounty with far-off relatives. It took an entire staff to run the program, but the company humanized the process by describing their gift packages in letters signed, "Dorothy Hudson, the Hudson Bay Company's "Personal Shopper."

"Order anything which we are able to supply from our

groceteria and we will pack and forward it for you," Dorothy wrote to the thousands who enquired about the parcels. The Bay made it even easier by offering pre-packaged assortment: the much prized $14-box of "Assortment Joan," which included sugar, two pounds of smoked bacon, tins of butter, cream, and chocolate. For a more modest $7.95, shoppers could order the "Assortment Betty." Thousands of these parcels were shipped out annually to loved ones in a long list of foreign countries. Finally, people from the Prairies had a little money to spare — and they spent it wisely.

"Dorothy Hudson" was not the only gift giver in those post-war years. Members of the Beaver Club, at the The Bay's Winnipeg Main street offices, packed up parcels of Canuck Christmas cheer for their HBC colleagues in "Old Blighty."

Inside the packages from Hudson's Bay House were novel Christmas cards. A large teepee Christmas card attracted a great deal of attention from the children attending the Christmas party in the staff canteen. One year, a plug-in Christmas tree card came complete with multi-coloured Christmas lights that twinkled through the cardboard. Another, a poster-sized effort, featured cartoon-like Canadian beavers hard at work at various wartime "essential services."

Lilian Leonard, the honorary secretary of the London Beaver Club, wrote to the Winnipeg gift-givers. "During the past week, we have felt rather like misers as your promised parcels started to arrive. At last, the whole 16 were here and so the members of the Committee experienced the great thrill of opening them and the pleasure of dividing up the cake and chocolates equally as most people wanted to take theirs home and share with their families. We created great excitement as we took round the gifts and felt just like Father Christmas."

Seasonal treats weren't all that recipients found nestled inside the boxes. More arcane items included real face-cloths; honest-to-goodness facecloths! It seems that HBC employees were tired of having to cut up old towels for their daily ablutions.

The staffers in London were quick to reciprocate, as best they could. Inside the parcels opened up on Main Street were "splendid and interesting ashtrays ... with descriptive plaques showing that they are made from stone of the Houses of Parliament damaged by enemy action in 1941," the Club's House Detective newsletter reported. Accompanying the unique ashtrays was a letter:

"A real bit of old London is our gift to you this year ... something useful as a token that London, at present battered and worn, will grow in usefulness and the London Beaver Club, now scattered and separated, will unite again in days of peace."

Prairie Prosperity Returns
By the late 1940s and into the mid-1950s, it appeared that the good times had returned at last. Canadian wheat was

king again, as it had been in the 1920s, when the Canadian Prairies were known as The Breadbasket of the Empire. By 1960, more than 80,000 combines reaped an average of 25 bushels an acre of the golden harvest the world clambered for. In the country, outhouses were disappearing as flush toilets were installed in even the most modest of farmhouses. Construction cranes swept the city skies over Regina, Calgary, and Winnipeg, as new, tall buildings reached upwards. There was even talk of an international airport in Edmonton.

Of course, there was no better time to celebrate the long-awaited good times than at Christmas. The gift-giving holiday was a made-to-order opportunity to celebrate new-found prosperity.

Oversized red felt Christmas stockings now replaced those long, dark woollen stockings or thick work socks that people might actually put their feet into the next day. These bright new stockings now hung heavy, bulging with promise. They were filled with little things kids never forgot: a Little Big Book (maybe Hopalong Cassidy), a miniature plastic game, bubble solution or a white lacrosse ball, doll clothes for the doll waiting under the tree, a small net-bag of marbles (cat's eyes, peeries and cobbs), a Dinky Toy army jeep, a package of baseball cards (maybe of Roy Campanella!) with that never-to-be forgotten scent of sweet-smelling gum, a kazoo or shiny silver whistle, wax lips, licorice pipes and candy cigarettes, a plastic ring, a skipping rope, Viewmaster reels of Little Lulu or The Lone Ranger, a set of jacks.

Special Gifts

And under the tree ...

Armies of lead soldiers, a Daisy air rifle (just like Red Ryder's), a Meccano set, a new Hardy Boys or Nancy Drew book, a Spin And Marty game, a walking-talking doll snuggled down in her own doll carriage. All marvellous stuff.

Thousands of grandparents who drove to Calgary or Winnipeg or Regina for Christmas dinner with the "kids" never thought they would live to see such prosperity. Some Christmas gifts were so big, they couldn't be shoved under the tree: a new hi-fi console, a big TV set, a new bedroom suite, all sorts of silvery gizmos for the bar in the basement rumpus room, honest-to-goodness power tools, the likes of which granddad had once seen only at lumberyards or furniture markers.

Santas Anonymous
However, "good-times Christmases" brought with them the sobering reminder that not everyone was able to celebrate in the modern, affluent way. In large cities, neighbour didn't always help neighbour as they once did in villages and small towns. (All too often, neighbour didn't even know neighbour.) Service clubs and what most people still called "the press" lent a hand.

The press now included radio and TV stations. In those pioneering days of rock-and-roll, radio in Edmonton meant CHED. Listening to CHED any weekday morning, anytime between 1955 and 1964, meant listening to John Barton.

"We really dominated the town," recalls John. "We did a lot of stuff nobody had ever thought about before."

One of the innovations the Edmonton station implemented in the late 1950s was a special Christmas charity program called Santas Anonymous, a concept that, in the decades since, has been implemented successfully in other cities and towns across Canada. John and other DJs took their cues from program manager Jerry Forbes.

"I don't know how the idea came up, but to the best of my knowledge, Jerry came up with the name," John explains. "Jerry and I sat down and we put the idea together. He said, 'wouldn't it be nice if people could donate gifts and remain anonymous?'"

Santas Anonymous remains today and is a unique way of helping those less fortunate. The main concept of the scheme, which made it so compelling, was that donations weren't cans of food left in boxes in grocery stores. They were gifts for children, given directly, one-to one, to the needy families.

"It became personal; it was a very personal way of giving." John remembers, explaining that donors could determine the gender and age of their recipients. "On the item, it would say, 'girl, seven to nine', or 'boy, twelve to fourteen', this sort of thing. Then, there was a blank card attached for the parent to sign as well, you know, 'from Mom' or 'from Santa'. And when we found out that a particular family had two boys and girl, we would package this up and it would be delivered to them."

Social agencies and church groups were delighted to provide names and addresses of needy recipients. John's role in all this, as the host of the morning show, was to sell the idea to the city, "bringing people on-board" during his shift and "in the commercials" he recorded later in the day. Not long after John went to work behind the microphone to promote the concept, the city's biggest radio listening audience began to respond. Then, others went to work behind the scenes.

"We had a huge space upstairs on the third floor of the radio station, and I remember staff and volunteers up there wrapping the gifts. It was very, very labour intensive." However, it was, in the true sense, a labour of love, and the labour was shared. When it was time to distribute the gifts, different groups in town volunteered to help.

The mountain of gifts was high enough that deliveries became a challenge and John became one of the many volunteer distributors. As Christmas approached, there was one more shopping bag left in the car, and one more name left on his list. One evening, John decided to make the last delivery, and he took along his six-year old son, Reid.

"I think I just brought him along for the ride, and I also thought, 'it's kind of a neat thing, you know.' I wasn't trying to teach him a lesson, but I just thought it would make Christmas mean a little bit more. The whole Santa Claus thing was just huge in his mind, and it was just a little difficult to explain to a six-year old, 'Well, why are you Santa?' So,

I probably said, 'well, Santa can't get to absolutely everybody and the odd person could possibly be missed.'"

When they got to the address, John asked his son to go to the house with him. Carrying the shopping bag full of parcels, John and Reid trudged through the snow and up the steps. "A woman came to the door and she had the little children around her. I explained to her that I was from Santas Anonymous. She immediately sent the little children off into another room to play because she knew the gifts were for them. We handed the gifts to the lady. There were tears in her eyes, and my son, I remember him looking around, and wondering why the little kids were gone, he really didn't know how to handle all this. It baffled him; you take so much for granted at that age. The woman cried; she hugged Reid and she hugged me, and thanked us very much, and said it was going to be a wonderful Christmas."

John and Reid got back into the car and started for home. Reid sat quietly, looking out the passenger-side window.

"Did you enjoy this evening?" John asked, finally.

"Yup."

A pause.

"So," John started. "You happy with everything?"

"Yeah."

"So, what's on your mind, right now?" John asked. Reid turned to his dad.

"The woman and her little girls," he said quietly. "How much she liked what we just did. I didn't know that everybody doesn't have a Christmas like we do."

"As a little child, he thought everybody was the same," says John. "That [visit] really hit him."

Chapter 6
Wild Wilderness Yuletides

C hristmas in Canada's "Wild West" was not represented by a single set of traditions or predictable components. The experience of Christmas varied depending on the circumstances, place, and perhaps most of all, time. Europeans arrived on the Prairies in the 18th century. The world — and the Canadian Prairies — changed enormously between the 1700s and the late 1800s. The very earliest prairie Christmases were enjoyed, or simply endured, in Manitoba.

Fur Trade Festivities
Fur was king. In what we now call Canada, two fur-trading dynasties, the Hudson's Bay Company and the North-West Company, did the king's bidding, constantly seeking out

new areas to bring under their commercial control. The West beckoned.

Inside the forts, which had been fashioned out of timbers by small groups of adventurer-fur traders, Christmas was usually celebrated somehow, if only with a single special dinner. Conditions were primitive in the vast wilds of Rupert's Land, so the fellowship and feasting of Christmas was welcomed.

The first recorded prairie Christmas was described in a short journal entry in 1715. The unknown record-keeper lived in Manitoba's oldest settlement, York Fort (later York Factory), located on the shores of Hudson Bay. He wrote: "Had prayers twice today as usual, and the men did have plentiful good victuals."

According to another diarist, Christmas wasn't that much different half a century later. "Spent the day with sobriety making merry with innocent diversions ... Mr. LaTower gave us his company to prayers but we make a poor hand of it for want of prayer books."

By 1800, new forts had been built. One, Fort Wedderburn, on the southwest shore of Lake Athabasca, was the home of George Simpson, governor of HBC in North America. On December 25, the governor wrote, "... the people had a dram in the morning and were allowed to make holyday. The gentlemen sat down to the most sumptuous Dinner that Fort Wedderburn could afford, true English fare, Roast Beef and plum pudding and afterwards a temperature Kettle of punch ..." And, as an afterthought, the governor added, "The weather was bitterly cold." He didn't say how cold it was, but an earlier entry in his Athabasca journal gives a hint. He wrote that, "within 4 feet of a large fire the Ink actually freezes in my pen."

Within 10 years, HBC had ceded a significant parcel of land, some 300,000 square kilometres, not for fur-trading endeavours, but "to establish agricultural settlers upon the lands." The recipient of the grant was Thomas Douglas, the fifth Earl of Selkirk. In 1812, Selkirk founded the Red River Colony. The grand gentleman did not lead the settlers himself, however. That task fell to his governor, Miles MacDonnell. It was no easy task in this wild country called Assiniboia, and, in the end, MacDonnell was replaced.

There was scarcely reason to celebrate Christmas during the first horrific years of the colony's life. Scurvy ravaged the men, and starvation threatened everyone. The first settlers were just glad to be alive. As conditions slowly improved, women and children joined the men. With their families in their midst, the men felt life was worth living again.

Inside the walls of stockaded communities, such as Fort Gibralter and Fort Daer, they celebrated Christmas with enthusiasm. In an 1812 journal entry, a gathering at the governor's residence at Daer is succinctly described: "We all dine at Mr. Hillier's. Dance to the Bag Pipe in the evening."

During the day, the men chose sides for Hurl, a game played by teams on the ice. The idea was to hit a ball with sticks and send it into the goal of the opposing team. Eighty years in the future, this primitive game played on a frozen river during the Christmas get-together at Fort Daer would be called hockey.

A few months after that Christmas, the colony was destroyed during a fur-trade war. Traders vied for land with farmers, and Nor'westers fought HBC personnel over trapping territory. By 1815, the first Red River Colony was a smouldering ruin.

The second colony fared much better. Five years later, the faithful were called to Christmas mass with church bells from two missions on either side of the river tolling out their message of peace and goodwill. Certainly, by this time, the colonists deserved a little of each. However, celebrations were premature. By the following Christmas, settlers were each rationed to a pint of wheat a day, which they boiled into a thin soup.

By 1830, after the amalgamation of the two huge fur empires, the lean, mean years were past, and Christmases were more bountiful. By the middle of the century, retired factors had made their home in Red River, now a settlement boasting 5000 souls.

More than 900 kilometres from any other settlement and 2400 kilometres from the nearest eastern city, the colonists were still isolated. Only the dog-trains provided a tenuous winter link with the outside world. However, Christmas was celebrated with tea-drinking, merry-making, and dancing to the lively sound of bows over fiddle-strings.

By the late 1840s, "civilization" had move west. At Fort Edmonton, artist and traveller Paul Kane sat down in the dining-hall to a 2 p.m. Christmas dinner with the others: the chief trader, clerks, and missionaries.

The artist wrote that the hall itself was a sight to behold, "painted in the style of the most startling barbaric gaudiness..." There was a reason for the garishness. The dining room doubled as reception room for visiting chiefs, and the decoration was undertaken, Kane concluded, simply to "astonish the natives."

No tablecloths, no fine cutlery, silver candelabra, or china, but "bright tin plates" on hardwood tables. And on those plates were turnips, potatoes, portions of boiled buffalo hump and buffalo tongue, and a very tender boiled, unborn buffalo calf. The menu was surprisingly varied, and diners enjoyed beaver tail, wild goose, dried moose nose, and white fish browned in buffalo marrow, followed by something called "mouffle."

"Let us drink to absent friends," was the typical toast of men seated around the table, men celebrating far away from homes and families. Another toast might follow, "To the ladies!" As an HBC clerk was to remark, during Christmas at York Factory, the "ladies" were among the "absent friends." The chief trader's wife was the only European woman present. In fact, she was the only white woman to be found within 400 kilometres of the fort.

Old Fort Edmonton, ca. 1900–1925

The high revelry of Christmas was carried out in the same manner in virtually all the major forts, and the typical fur-trade yuletide celebration became a tradition unto itself. As the 20th century dawned, and the major forts — Garry, Calgary, and Edmonton — became cities, fur-trade Christmas traditions had all but passed into history.

In the early 1920s, Philip Godsell, an HBC post inspector, was sent north by the company on a fact-finding expedition. Godsell travelled more than 1,200 kilometres by dog team, inspecting the posts and reorganizing the books. His journey took him through Fort Simpson, throughout the Great Slave Lake area, and into the Arctic. While travelling, he uncovered, as he put it, "the most flagrant dishonesty and incompetency..."

Godsell was more than a bookkeeper. He was a romantic. He realized he was living in what we would now call a "time warp." He experienced what few living Canadians ever had, and he wrote about it — prolifically. As well as writing numerous hair-raising Canadian wilderness stories for pulp magazines, he tapped out melodramatic crime and adventure tales such as "Vengeance of the Mounted," "Death Stalks the Night," and dozens of other stories, most of which have a firm foundation in fact.

He also wrote about the last vestiges of the fur-trade's Christmas Day fun. He, along with many others, travelled miles to the main fort for an occasion that served as one part tribal reunion and one part Christmas celebration:

"Hitching my L'Assumption belt around my fringed buckskin capote, I cracked the whip and, in a flash, my five rangey huskies sprang into their collars and we were off." And so begins Godsell's story, *Yuletide Trail*, a tale similar to the writer's other seasonal stories, "Christmas Comes To Norway House," and "Christmas on the Frozen Frontier."

Godsell had a talent for marketing and a zeal for self-promotion. He referred to himself as "one of America's outstanding authorities on the Indians and the Far North." He had his photo taken in Plains Indian regalia or in fur-trapper garb. His adoption of the racy style of the 30s "pulps" tend now to cast doubt on the veracity of his stories. Yet, despite stilted dialogue and florid descriptions, Godsell paints a fascinating picture of how it probably was:

"Hardly had we finished supper of horned owl soup, roast venison and an enormous but anaemic plum pudding ere a rattle of gunfire announced that the Christmas ball was underway. Immediately, the house was thrown into a furor of excitement as Helen [the trader's Native wife], accompanied by a wave of dusky femininity, surged out into the courtyard and headed for the Indian House. A huge plume of smoke arose from the mud chimney and the windows glowed redly as we plunged in and out of the cold. At the far end, two per-spiring fiddlers, squatted on upturned packing-cases, were thumping their moccasined feet to the squealing strains of the music. The fun was fast and furious; Indians laughed in happy abandon, squaws giggled, and young bucks howled with delight as they swung their partners off their feet. With wild enthusiasm, Eightsome Reel followed Ribbit Dance, Drops o' Brandy, the riotous handkerchief dance and the inevitable and oft-repeated Red River Jig. Then came a midnight supper of boiled muskrats, baked beaver, moose ribs, and bannock with strong black tea to revive flagging energies; and so the fun and frolic continued till the first rosy blush of dawn."

Writing about January 1, Godsell told his readers that nobody was in condition to stir until late in the afternoon.

"Then, one by one, trappers, traders and Indians hitched up their dog teams, loaded their toboggans, slipped moccasined feet into snowshoe thongs and struck out along snowy trails that led to the heart of the wilderness."

Christmas During "The Troubles"

"The troubles." That's what people called the 1869 Riel Rebellion. Those particular troubles had been brewing for some time. There was fear and concern among the Métis people, the hardy prairie hunters of mixed French and Native blood. How could they safeguard their land? With the impending transfer of Rupert's Land, which included much of western Canada and the Red River Settlement to the Dominion of Canada, things started to happen fast.

First, the Métis leader, Louis Riel, formed a provisional government. Then the new government imprisoned 63 Canadians who, at the request of Governor Macdougall, had taken up arms as a show of strength against the Métis.

For those 63 men who were imprisoned, life was not so much nerve-wracking as boring. The meals were meagre: boilers full of hot tea and bread in the morning, and boiled beef and bread at noon. But now that Christmas was approaching, they hoped for a decent meal. However, food was not their main concern. They wanted to go home. The day before Christmas, one wrote, "Hoped to be released today, but were disappointed. One of the boys got hold of a violin and tonight there is music and dancing. Some of the guards came in and danced with us."

On Christmas Day, there was no breakfast. The prisoners were discouraged, then worried: what did this mean? What it meant was that women in the nearby village were trying to prepare Christmas dinner for them, but distance was making it difficult. The Fort Garry jail was more than a kilometre away from the housewives' homes. At last, as evening approached, a tasty meal was delivered to the jail. One prisoner wrote the following:

"Mr. Crowson brought in roast beef, plum pudding and tarts. We have few friends in town (as all who could do so have moved their families to remoter parts), but what we have are very mindful of us. I believe we are indebted for tonight's dinner to Miss Drever, Mrs. Crowson, and Mr. Alex McArthur. Long may they live! Music and dancing tonight."

The following year, General Garnet Wolseley led Canadian and British troops to the colony to put down the rebellion. Riel fled, and the rebellion was over. The next Christmas, Wolseley's forces were still in the Fort — much to their consternation. They had been unhappy since their arrival in Fort Garry; not only had Riel disappeared, so had the supplies. Naturally enough, the quartermaster sergeant took the brunt of their displeasure. Christmas dinner loomed. The quartermaster sergeant was in a quandary. What could he serve them for dinner? He came up with a plan.

When the soldiers trooped into the dining hall, they were greeted by a wonderful sight. Beef boiled, beef soup, beef roasted and stewed! The laughing, joking men ate their fill. Eventually, the quartermaster sergeant got to his feet.

"Gentlemen, have I satisfied you at last?"

"You have!" they roared.

"Is there one man here present who is not perfectly, absolutely satisfied?"

"No, not one," came the cheers.

"The dinner was a great, a noble success?"

"It was!"

"Would you like it repeated tomorrow?"

As the rousing cheers died down, the smiling Quartermaster turned to his assistant and said, "The best thing we can do, Hank, is to go down and get the rest of that old horse."

There was a sudden stampede out the doors in the direction of the latrines.

The Other Men in Red

Beginning in 1874, a new kind of fort was being constructed on the Canadian Prairies: the North-West Mounted Police post. Once again, men were leaving family and friends behind and making the trip out west, which they called the North-west Territories. The "long march," which began in Dufferin, Manitoba, was gruelling enough, but once various troops reached their destination, their work began in earnest. There were forts to build, Native peoples to meet and impress, and whiskey traders to run to ground and arrest.

Much that we know of these days we owe to a handful of men who, either through their letters and diaries or through later reminiscences, related their experiences. One of those men was Richard Nevitt. He and his family had escaped the American Civil War by leaving Savannah, Georgia, when he was a small boy. They'd settled in Ontario, where Nevitt later entered the University of Toronto and obtained his Bachelor of Medicine.

He had to leave university before he became a qualified doctor, because his family could no longer support him. Nevitt knew he had to find a job, but his choices were few. Luckily, he was offered a position that would enable him to earn enough money to complete his education. It would also give him some unique experiences. He accepted a position as an assistant surgeon to the North-West Mounted Police, and joined them in Manitoba for the March West. Christmas found him at the newly constructed Fort Macleod, where Christmas Day was observed as a "Holyday." Nevitt watched policeman as they set to work creating festive mottos to be hung about the officers' mess: "Law and Order Is Peace And Prosperity" and "Nor'West Mounted Police, Pioneers of a Glorious Future."

It seems, in addition to other things, Christmas Day was an occasion to impress the area's Native people. That morning, the captain fired a few rounds from a howitzer, using a tree as a target. He was warming up for the big show to come. At 2 p.m., the Blackfoot arrived at the fort and the police and

Christmas dinner, Royal Canadian Mounted Police,
"K" division mess, Edmonton, Alberta, 1934.

Natives all went out onto the prairie so the Mounties could demonstrate the deadly accuracy of long-range artillery. With each roar of the howitzer, it was obvious that the "Pioneers of a Glorious Future" were going to ensure "peace and prosperity" through a strategy of persuasion by firepower.

After the demonstration, they rode back to the fort, where the Blackfoot enjoyed a "coffee break," with biscuits, rice, and molasses. After the Blackfoot left, it was time for the officers to enjoy Christmas dinner with their men.

On the menu that December 25, 1874 was roast hare,

roast beef, and haunch of venison. After the plum pudding, out came the whiskey and talk of "Christmases gone by, of friends and home." At 11 p.m. the party moved to B Troop for dancing and a concert. An hour or so later, the officers visited the quarters of F Troop for a midnight supper of "oysters, canned fruit, pies, rice pudding, plum pudding and lots of it." The night was young! An interpreter was sent to bring local Natives in for more dancing and "we gave them some supper, and 4 o'clock saw the end of Christmas Day."

Everyone, Nevitt admitted, expected to have a gloomy time out on the primitive prairie, but the "united efforts of men and officers managed to dispel the gloom."

But dispelling the gloom, as Nevitt put it, was more difficult for the women. One reason was the lack of just about anything that made a house a home — at Christmas or any other time.

In what is now southern Alberta, supplies came about once a month from Fort Benton, Montana. Mrs. George Jacques, who "kept house" in a one-room log hut with sod roof and mud floor, waited at least that long for a stove. Not that she had anything much to cook on it. There were a few canned potatoes, and bread and meat. That was Christmas dinner, and most other dinners, as well.

Elizabeth McDougall, the second wife of Reverend John McDougall, a pioneering cleric who established Methodist missions in Edmonton, Calgary, and Fort McLeod, had a similar problem. "We had buffalo meat and bread and I believe

I managed to make some sort of pudding with flour, buffalo suet and Saskatoon berries," she wrote. "People wonder how we managed to cook without butter or eggs but somehow we did. I used the soft fat from around the spleen of the buffalo for shortening."

Tragedy at Christmas

The frigid temperatures and rough conditions of prairie winters often brought untimely death to the early settlers.

Thirty kilometres south of Fort Macleod, down the Old Man River, a small NWMP detachment had made a winter home in an abandoned whiskey post called Fort Kipp. Two of the men there, Baxter and Wilson, had been given leave, and spent it upriver at Fort Macleod. After a fine time at Christmas, they left the fort and started their trip back to their detachment.

That same day, at Fort Macleod, news arrived that a bull team had reached Fort Whoop-Up (near today's Lethbridge) with supplies and mail for the policemen. Officer Cecil Denny asked the colonel if he could ride to Whoop-Up and bring back the mail, the first letters since the start of the long march in June! Colonel Macleod hesitated, then gave his permission.

Denny was halfway to Whoop-Up when the blizzard hit. He turned back to Fort Macleod but, as he later wrote, "with the wind and snow full in my face ... I had difficulty in keeping my eyelids from freezing together." In desperation,

Denny changed direction and headed to Fort Kipp instead. He would have frozen to death had it not been for his long, warm buffalo coat, and his horse. Still he suffered: "I only saved myself from freezing by dismounting at intervals and running beside the horse." It got worse when darkness fell. Running beside the horse was no longer an option. Denny remounted, not daring to leave the saddle, and let the horse have his head, trusting that his mount could find his way somehow. The horse and his trusting rider ploughed on through the snowdrifts for hours.

"Then suddenly I found myself surrounded by lighted windows. Without my realizing it, the horse had walked through the open gate of Fort Kipp and stopped in the middle of the square."

Incredibly, after his horrific ordeal, Denny got back on his horse the very next day and rode out to Whoop Up and back without incident, carrying the precious mail to news-starved policemen. He was not the first arrival. During his absence, two rider-less horses had stumbled into the fort — the mounts Baxter and Wilson had been riding. Police and Natives saddled up and rode out to search for the missing men. A few hours later, they brought them back. Baxter was frozen stiff, and Wilson was close to death. Denny raced to Fort Macleod to fetch Richard Nevitt. They returned to find that the badly frozen Wilson had already expired.

Blinded by the snow, the two hapless men had circled aimlessly in the whiteout, and then, exhausted, had made a critical mistake: they'd decided to rest for a while. They dismounted, lay down, and allowed the freezing temperature to claim them.

Christmas Day Pastimes

By the late 1860s, it was obvious that the focus of life was moving from inside the forts to the surrounding settlements. In 1867 a cathedral — actually a small log structure — was being built in St. Albert, near Fort Edmonton. Even though the structure was only half finished at Christmas, the settlers flocked there for midnight mass, leaving Fort Edmonton deserted that night. As befitting the time and place, Christmas hymns were sung in Cree. The priest followed suit with a Cree-language service.

Today, many people play games or take part in some kind of sport on Christmas Day. This is not a new idea. Our prairie forefathers spent their Christmases taking part in buffalo hunts (out of Fort Edmonton), toasting Jesus with whiskey at church (at Fort Pitt), going on rabbit shooting expeditions (around Fort Saskatchewan), or taking part in overland races (at Fort Macleod). One year, during one of Alberta's famous chinooks, when there wasn't a patch of snow left on the ground, a storm blew up right in the middle of an overland race. One observer reported that when the runners hit the home stretch, "You couldn't see anything for dust."

As years passed, Christmas customs reflected a more civilized tone. The HBC offered a special bachelor's hamper, which simplified the Christmas gift-giving decisions. For $5, friends could order a hamper that included all the necessities of prairie life: rye, scotch, port, claret, and a box of cigars. The hampers had another advantage: they promoted 19th century social "networking." The giver usually visited the recipient sooner, rather than later, to sample some of the gift!

Chapter 7

The True Spirit of Christmas

gaily decorated tree, the familiar strains of festive songs, and the mouth-watering aroma of baking are all part of Christmas. But the holiday season is frequently made special by something else — something that we can't see, hear, or smell. It is the special word or deed shared, either unexpectedly or spontaneously, with friends, family, or strangers. These acts of warm-hearted generosity embody what we call the Sprit of Christmas. That spirit lives on in our hearts long after the material trappings of Christmas have been put away for another year.

A Hold-up, High jinks, and Humanity

The spirit of Christmas means, among other things, joy.

The True Spirit of Christmas

There was plenty of joy within Calgary's large King family. In her evocative book, *The House With The Light On*, Horace King's daughter, Eleanor King Byers, shares many whimsical and touching Christmas stories that tell us much about the Christmas spirit.

Say the words, "Tea Kettle Inn" to long-time Calgary residents over the age of 50 and watch their eyes light up. Run by Horace King and his sister, Millie Snowden, the 7th Avenue restaurant was, during the 1930s, 40s, and 50s, one of the city's finest dining spots. The inn, located next door to the Kings' House of Antiques, boasted "Delicious Meals of Quality prepared by expert Lady Cooks." It was no idle boast. A bevy of uniformed waitresses served prime rib, chicken pot-pie, and real tea made from real tea leaves, poured from real china teapots.

One Saturday evening in December, business, as usual, was brisk at the Tea Kettle. Horace and Millie had already gone home to their families, leaving their staff to look after the last diners and close the restaurant. Near closing time, a solitary man walked in. The silent stranger didn't pull up a chair and sit down at a table. Instead, he walked right up to the cashier and pulled out a gun.

The terrified cashier didn't hesitate. She emptied the till and handed over the cash. The robber grabbed the bank notes and simply walked quickly out of the restaurant. Once the door closed behind him, pandemonium reigned. It took only a few seconds for one plucky waitress to jump over the counter and give chase. A short time later, she staggered into the restaurant, gasping for breath. She was empty-handed. After pursuing the thief for blocks, she had finally given up.

Horace was upset about the incident, but in the swirl of pre-Christmas activity, he didn't waste too much time thinking about it. However, two days before Christmas, someone jogged his memory.

On returning home from shopping, the Kings found a large cardboard box on the front porch. From the top of the box, a wooden pole pointed skywards. Perplexed, they climbed the steps to take a closer look. Attached to the box was a note that read: THIS IS A STICK-UP. It was a pre-Christmas "present" from Eleanor's cousins.

This kind of joke was typical of the King family. They enjoyed high jinks and imaginative shenanigans, especially at Christmas. One year, another uncle, Harry, mischievously invited his kids and their cousins to "go fishing" for Christmas presents. He led them to the kitchen, where a bed sheet concealed a corner of the room, and ducked behind the sheet. Meanwhile, Eleanor's aunt, Lil, handed out "fishin' poles" (sticks tied with string "line" and safety-pin "hooks"). When the fishing lines sailed across the top of the sheet, Harry put little presents onto the hooks for each of the yuletide anglers, announcing each "catch" with a sharp tug.

At one of the Tea Kettle's staff Christmas parties, it was the same Uncle Harry who announced a "Guess the Baby's Weight" contest. He collected all the guesses, then, not content to simply tell the party-goers the correct weight, he carefully lifted real, live, four-month-old Audrey King onto the restaurant's big butcher scales.

For other parties, Horace King wrote inspirational plays that cast waitresses, cooks, and others in such roles as Humility, Forgiveness, and Charity. There were lessons, as well as laughter, to share.

Horace King was a generous man who actively sought out and helped needy people. Eleanor remembers delivering food, clothing, and toys to families who had fallen on hard times. One repeat recipient of Horace's charity was the reclusive Miss Moss, a lady who lived in a weather-beaten, dilapidated house across from what is now Memorial Park. She rarely ventured out of her house, even to go shopping. Instead, she hired neighbours to get her groceries and do the outside chores. Her instructions were always the same: take the groceries around the back, please. Nobody — except Horace — had ever seen the inside of her house.

Horace called on Miss Moss every Christmas Eve to deliver a turkey dinner with all the trimmings, compliments of the Kings and the folks at the Tea Kettle. Significantly, Horace was granted a front-door entrance. All he asked in return was that she leave the empty tray on the porch for Boxing Day pick-up. Naturally, Horace's kids were curious about the old woman's house. Eleanor and her brother Don begged repeatedly to be taken along when he took the dinner tray.

One Christmas Eve, Horace relented. He warned the

two that they might be left standing out on the porch, and to "accept her choice graciously." Wonder of wonders, Miss Moss let them all in. Once inside, the brother and sister stared at "a lifetime of newspapers, periodicals and nondescript collectibles stockpiled from floor to ceiling."

Eleanor remembers that Horace urged the old lady to get outside more often. She also remembers Miss Moss telling Horace that she had taken a walk in the park the previous July, "veiled, of course."

On Boxing Day, when the Kings' car pulled up in front of the old house, the Tea Kettle tray was waiting on Miss Moss's front porch, as usual. There was no note of thanks or belated Christmas card. None was expected. The tray was empty, and that was reward enough for Horace King.

The Old Toy Truck Rolls Again

June Cox, who was brought up in Saskatoon, Saskatchewan, during the Depression, remembers her childhood Christmases fondly. Although money was tight, she and her brother Bob would always get one, perhaps two, Christmas presents. She still remembers many of her own special gifts, but it was one of Bob's gifts that left an indelible impression on them both.

Like Jim Storey's Christmas morning surprise a decade earlier in nearby Dundurn, this, too, was a metal dump truck. And like Jim's, this was no ordinary truck. "It was big... I would say sixteen, seventeen inches long. And it was sturdy. I can remember the little kids would sit on it! And, for us to have it, in the Depression! I have no idea how my parents afforded it," says June.

One December, years after Bob had stopped playing with the truck, June's father asked Bob if they could give the toy to someone else. A new family had moved into a nearby house the summer before. It didn't take long for neighbours to realize that the family was in trouble. "I think the father was alcoholic; I don't think he had a job," June recalls. "They had three or four kids. Dad said, 'You know, what about that little guy down at the end of the street? The youngest one. Do you think he'd like this?' And that's when they decided to fix up the truck."

After years of hauling and dumping at the miniature construction sites that dotted the empty lots around the family's house, the truck was looking worn. Its original blue paint was faded, and the enamel-like finish was chipped. Much cleaning, sanding, and scraping ensued. The paint can was pried open, and that dull blue disappeared under a coat of bright red paint. Then Father and son had another great idea.

One of the most popular toys young boys had at the time was a spring-loaded popgun, the kind that fired harmless corks. Out from a corner of the bedroom closet came Bob's half-forgotten toy weapon. "I remember they painted the stock brown, and spruced it up, too," June says.

Upstairs, June and her mother were busy making popcorn balls. Would the kids at the end of the street like some of those? Another great idea!

Finally, the gun, truck, and popcorn balls were ready. What now? Their parents looked down at them and smiled. Uh-oh. Brother and sister glanced at each other. It had all been great fun up until this moment. The kids hadn't considered the delivery part of the scheme; they thought that their parents would somehow take care of that. Now it was up to them!

The two didn't know much about the intended recipients; nobody seemed to. "The family was ... well, different. The kids were different. Of course they were!" June says emphatically. "Their upbringing was entirely different from ours."

Nevertheless, arms full, out the door they went. Things got tense as June and Bob approached the neighbours' yard. June laughs at the memory. "I remember we looked at each other and Bob whispered nervously, 'Should we knock? Should we stay at the door?'" They shook their heads. That was asking too much! Brother and sister held their breath, crept up the stairs, and placed their presents at the front door.

"And then we just ran!"

The warm glow created by the incident lingered for years.

"I can always remember my brother being so impressed with that Christmas. He just thought that was the best Christmas." It wasn't what he received that year that remained in Bob's memory. It was, June maintains, what he had given up.

The True Spirit of Christmas

The Extra Hamper

It was 1935 and, according to the calendar, Christmas was just around the corner. Yet, for many Depression-era households, Christmas might never have come at all if it hadn't been for the generosity of others. For thousands of families, Christmas actually arrived with an unexpected knock at the door. The door would open to reveal a smiling stranger standing on the porch with a shopping bag in his hand, or with arms wrapped around a large cardboard box.

"Merry Christmas," he would say. "Merry Christmas from Rotary." Or the Lions. Or the Legion. Then, gesturing at the bag, "Here's something for the kids ..." or, "Christmas dinner, Ma'am."

Calgary's Archdeacon Cecil Swanson, or "Swanny" as he was known, told many touching tales of Christmas generosity. One particular story concerned two men who somehow found themselves with an extra Christmas hamper.

As they had before, Harry and his friend Pete were bringing a little Christmas to needy folks living in the small wooden houses not far from downtown Calgary. That December in 1935, hefting the Club Christmas hampers into and out of the car, climbing flights of stairs, and standing on tiny porches was cold, hard work. But the two men didn't mind. Their shivering stopped when they felt the warmth of abashed smiles and choked murmurs of thanks from grateful men and women.

Harry and Pete were just saying goodbye to the lady at

the last home on their list when they remembered the last hamper, an extra hamper, sitting on the floor behind the front seat of the car. They asked the woman if there was another family nearby that might appreciate a little "Christmas," too. She pointed up the street, in the direction of a home of new neighbours. Three or four children, she thought.

The pair thanked her for the tip and went to the house. Harry and Pete took one look inside the home, at the bare wooden floors, the shabby furniture, and the hollow-eyed youngsters, and instantly knew their extra hamper was going to make a big difference.

How many kids? they asked. The mother held up four fingers. Harry looked around. There was dad, and three youngsters. "Okay, where's number four?" he laughed.

"Oh, he's in the shed," the father replied nonchalantly.

"In the shed? Harry exclaimed in surprise. There was something about the furtive, hesitant look in the father's eyes. "Where's the shed?" Harry asked.

"I'll show you."

While Pete helped the mother empty the hamper, the father led Harry through the kitchen. There, attached crudely to the back of the house itself, was a small plank lean-to, scarcely bigger than a bathroom. Inside the lean-to was a narrow bed. And there, nestled beneath the old blankets, white and wan, lay a little boy.

Harry swallowed hard and approached the bed. He had seen that look before. He knew what it meant: tuberculosis. A terrible life-threatening illness for anyone who contracted it, TB also instilled a terrible fear in those close to the afflicted. Harry knew that fear all too well; he remembered the strict instructions, the boiling, bubbling water in which bed sheets were washed, and the warnings not to share drinking glasses, cutlery, or even a kiss. Harry had been a TB victim, too. He gave the boy a warm smile and then led his father aside.

"I'll be back Wednesday morning," he said quietly. The father looked up and nodded wordlessly.

As Harry turned the ignition in the car, he told Pete what he had seen. He had an idea, he said, and then, before he pulled out onto the silent, snow-covered street, he told Pete not to tell a soul. But sometime later, Pete told "Swanny" because the story was too wonderful not to share.

The following Wednesday, as promised, Harry arrived back at the house. He had a carpenter with him. Two days later, a new, bigger, brighter lean-to had been built, one with a large glass window. Also, Harry had furnished it with a new bed and new warm, colourful blankets. Later, a doctor arrived to check the boy. It was the first of many visits.

Generosity comes in many forms. In this case, it was a food hamper and $1800 worth of labour, materials, and medical care. But the "gift" was a gift of hope to a sick boy and his frightened family.

Seeing the Light
As a young boy growing up in Edmonton in the late 1920s,

Frank Mould often noticed his mother's acts of generosity. From her example, he learned the value of giving; from one of the people she befriended, he learned another valuable lesson.

"You know how, as a kid, you'll get fascinated by a man who's blind?" Frank asks. "This guy, his name was Horace Fawcett, lived down on the flats. He was quite amazing. He was blind from birth. I can remember, as a kid, seeing him come down the street with his white cane. And the way that son-of-a-gun just knew when he was going to reach the sidewalk was something."

Even more amazing for Frank and many others was the fact that the blind man became a door-to-door salesman for Watkins products. Making a decent living, however, was a challenge for the sightless. Horace lived modestly. He also lived alone. In those days, being blind meant living in isolation.

"He was befriended by my mother," Frank recalled, "to the point that he was almost a member of the family. At Christmastime, I'd be sent down to his house to take him a plum pudding that mother had made. He would open the door and I'd sit down. Then he'd say, 'Oh, Frank! It's pretty dark in this house, let me put the lights on so we can see what we're doing!'"

The lesson young Frank learned from his blind neighbour was to take life's challenges in stride and laugh at your troubles.

Ridin' the Rods

They called it "ridin' the rods." The "rods" might be those tracks that snaked away from Banff, or led into Edmonton, cut through Regina, or ran in and out of the huge CPR marshalling yards in the centre of Winnipeg. It could have been 1930, or '33, or '36. Whatever the place, whatever the year, there was no Merry Christmas for these men; bitter, destitute men on their way to ... anywhere.

They were the hobos, the vagrants, the tramps and troublemakers, the unemployed thousands without homes, the kind of homes they watched speed by as the long freights sped away from 'the peg' on the CPR main line. Homes of ordinary families — homes like that of the Payjacks'...

Just a few blocks away from "CPR town," close enough that you could hear the long, low mournful sound of the train whistle, the family was gathering inside the Payjack house. It was Christmas Day and aunts, uncles, and cousins were at the table eating dinner. They were happy. They knew how fortunate they were. They had a warm, roomy house — not like those mean-looking shacks closer to the yards. There was a wage earner in this house, so in spite of hardship all around, there was plenty to celebrate.

Because this was a family gathering, they were surprised to hear a knock at the door. Mr. Payjack answered the knock, wondering who could possibly be calling on this day of days. There, on the veranda, stood a teenager. Collar turned up against the cold, face and hands streaked with grime, he looked a sad sight. Shivering, the boy asked if he could have something to eat — or maybe a little something so he could buy a bite somewhere.

Mr. Payjack immediately invited him in. Living so close to the rail yards and depot, he could guess the boy's story; he had seen others like him before. First the boy was led to the bathroom. A few minutes later, he emerged with a clean face and hands, and wearing a clean shirt. An extra place was set at the table, and he was asked to join them for dinner.

After the last relative had left, Mrs. Payjack made up a bed on the chesterfield. It must have felt like a cloud under the young vagabond's bruised and weary body. In the morning, the Payjacks gave him some warm clothing, a lunch of Christmas leftovers, and a gift of folding money. There were handshakes and good luck wishes, and the boy disappeared around the house and out of their lives.

Many years later, Mrs. Payjack answered the door to find another stranger standing on the veranda. The smiling man greeted her and asked to see her husband. The middle-aged woman shook her head sadly and told him that her husband had passed away some years ago. To her surprise, the man began to weep. Regaining his composure, the caller reminded her of a Christmas Day many years before, and of her husband's generosity towards a hungry, homeless young hobo who had been riding the rods.

During the years he had spent struggling up from poverty, the boy had never forgotten that unhesitating gesture of goodwill on that long-ago Christmas Day. Now, he had returned to say thank you. Not knowing what else to do, he pulled some money from his wallet and offered it to Mrs. Payjack. She thanked him for the offer but refused to accept it.

"That's the way my husband would want it to be," she explained.

Nodding, the young man thanked her and said a final goodbye. The Payjacks never saw him again. Except, of course, in their memories when they thought about that Christmas when a homeless young man shared their Christmas dinner.

You Can't Steal Christmas

Like so many of his contemporaries, Ron Hayter, a Saskatoon alderman, grew up when times were lean. "We were a poor family, hacking a living out of the northeastern Saskatchewan forest," he told *Saskatoon Star Phoenix* readers in a 1972 feature entitled, *Cornerstones of Christmas*. "My father's pulpwood camp was located at Akosane, one of those tiny CNR flag stops that have long since vanished. It was only eleven miles from the town of Hudson Bay, but we were often isolated by unpredictable bush roads."

Ron was the oldest child at the time, and the kids were all convinced that this would be "our best Christmas ever." One of the reasons for the optimism was that Ron's father was expecting payment for a shipment of pulpwood. On Christmas Eve day, he announced to the family that he had decided they would all go to Hudson Bay in the half-ton. Everyone was excited. Who wouldn't be? There was a COD parcel from Eaton's waiting at the post office.

After picking up the precious parcel, they began shopping in earnest. Bag after bag — including one that contained a big, fat turkey — went into the truck. Finally, with a farewell look at the Christmas lights of "downtown" Hudson Bay, the Hayters drove home.

They had barely walked in and turned the coal oil lamps on when dad followed them in, his face as dark as a thundercloud. Some things were missing from the back of the truck. What? "Things," as in turkey, groceries — and even the parcel from Eaton's. Everything had been stolen.

Ron's father turned around and headed back to Hudson Bay immediately. He woke up the butcher who lived at the rear of the grocery store. There were no turkeys left. Not even a chicken. He came back empty-handed.

On Christmas morning, the only gifts under the tree were handmade mittens, the usual gift from Grandma on Prince Edward Island, and the few other little gifts the boys had made for each other and their parents.

However, this was Christmas, and Mom was darned if everyone was going to mope around the house all day. She took the disappointed boys aside and gave them a kindly lecture. Yes, someone took things out of our truck, she said. But think about it; whoever took those packages needs them worse than we do. So what was Christmas about, anyway?

Wasn't the real spirit of Christmas giving? Wasn't giving more important than receiving? As the boys looked at her solemnly, she ended her lecture with, "Let's hope they have a very merry Christmas."

"She made us understand," Ron wrote, "She was good at that."

The Hayters didn't have turkey that Christmas. They didn't have those shiny new presents from Eaton's. They didn't have any nuts, fruit, or candy. However, Christmas dinner was another thing.

Ron's father took out the shotgun and Mom and the kids watched him drive away in the truck. Later that day, he was back with Christmas dinner — enough plump partridges to feed two families! Mom stuffed the birds with savoury sage dressing and put them in the oven to roast. They were delicious. The tasty meal was followed by a steam pudding with caramel sauce and some wonderful homemade fudge.

"I didn't get the gun and holster set, or the windup tractor, that I longed for," Ron wrote, "But, somehow, I remember that Christmas as being one of the most significant in my life. And one of the happiest."

Bibliography

Berton, Pierre. *The Dionne Years*. Toronto: McClelland & Stewart Ltd., 1977.

Bruce, Jean. *The Last Best West*. Publishing Centre, Minister of Supply And Services Canada, 2000.

Byers, Eleanor King. *The House With The Light On*. Calgary: Eleanor King Byers, 2003.

Charyk, John C. *The Biggest Day Of The Year*. Saskatoon: Western Producer Prairie Books, 1985.

Comstock, Eileen. *Sunny Side Up*. Calgary: Fifth House Publishers, 2001.

Dempsey, Hugh. *A Christmas In The West*. Saskatoon: Western Producer Prairie Books, 1982.

Hayes, John L. *Where Did You Come From*. Vancouver: John L Hayes, 1997.

Hayter, Ron. "Cornerstones of Christmas." *Saskatoon Star Phoenix* , Dec. 23, 1972.

Bibliography

Holmes, Peggy. *It Could Have Been Worse*. Toronto: Collins Publishers, 1980.

Leslie, Jean. *Glimpses of Calgary Past*. Calgary: Detselig Entertainment, 1994.

Moore, Alice, *Big Coulee School – Teacher's Eye-view, in Clover and Wild Strawberries*. Calgary: Friesen Printers, 1967.

Morris, Myrna L. "My Visit With Santa." *Fort Qu'Appelle Times*, Dec. 22, 1982.

Roger, Gertrude Minor. *Lady Rancher*. Saanichton: Hancock House Publishers Ltd., 1979.

Acknowledgements

This writer, and indeed, all prairie people, owe a special debt of gratitude to a number of authors who have kept the spirit of Christmas alive in their reminiscences and in collections of Yuletide anecdotes and stories.

In particular, two men of letters — one a teacher, the other a recognized Alberta historian — deserve special acknowledgement and thanks. John Charyk, a long-time teacher and member of the Alberta Foundation for the Literary Arts, was the editor of the anthology, *The Biggest Day Of The Year*, a fascinating and warm-hearted examination of the school Christmas concert. Hugh A. Dempsey, former assistant director of Calgary's Glenbow Museum and recipient of the Order of Canada, created, with his book, *Christmas In The West*, a treasury of Christmas stories that span the first 150 years of Prairie habitation. The author owes much to these two authors and their collections.

Mention should be made of the publisher of these two works, Western Producer Prairie Books of Saskatoon. Western Producer, was, by its own description, "a unique publishing venture owned by a group of prairie farmers who are members of Saskatchewan Wheat Pool," dedicated to preserving and popularizing the history and culture of prairie people.

My thanks to Eleanor King Byers, whose self-published

autobiographical book, *The House With the Light On*, chronicles the life and times of Calgary's entrepreneurial King family and its popular Tea Kettle Inn. The book is a special delight and I am grateful to be able to include some of Eleanor's Christmas memories in this Amazing Stories volume.

Episodes recounted in two other books became the inspiration for stories in this volume. *Ridin' the Rods* is originally told in *Sunny Side Up*, one of a number of warmhearted reminiscences by the late Eileen Comstock. *The Lost Gift* and *Santa Outdone* are based on an autobiographical incident related in Jean Leslie's *Glimpses of Calgary Past*.

My special thanks to all those who shared their personal prairie Christmas memories with me.

Thanks also to the helpful staff of the Glenbow Archives, Winnipeg's Hudson's Bay Company Archives, and Banff's Whyte Museum and Archives.

Photo Credits

Cover: courtesy The Estate of William Kurelek and The Isaacs Gallery, Toronto; Glenbow Archives: pages 28 (NA-2483-7), 36 (NA-3550-25), 102 (NA-3409-13); National Archives of Canada: page 95 (Charles W. Mathers / PA-031760); collection of Kara Turner: page 72.

About the Author

BC-born author Rich Mole has enjoyed an eclectic communications career, as a former broadcaster, a freelance journalist, and, for 20 years, the president of a successful Vancouver Island advertising agency. A lifelong fascination with history has fuelled his desire to write about the times and people of Canada's past. Rich now makes his home in Calgary, Alberta.